ANTIQUE
STYLE

ANTIQUE
STYLE

MAGGIE PHILO

AURUM

First published in Great Britain in 2000
by Aurum Press Ltd
25 Bedford Avenue, London WC1B 3AT

Project Editor: Heather Dewhurst
Designer: Kit Johnson
Photography: David Johnson and Jon Bouchier
Styling: Karina Garrick

A catalogue record for this book is available
from the British Library.

ISBN 1 85410 656 2

10 9 8 7 6 5 4 3 2 1

2004 2003 2002 2001 2000

Printed in Hong Kong/China
by South China Printing Co (1988) Ltd.

Contents

Introduction

Recently there have been a number of books produced which illustrate how to give old junk a new look and I thought it was time there was one where new projects are given an old and time-worn appearance. There are many advantages to decorating new items, but perhaps the most important of these, with many of us leading busy lives, is the huge saving in time. While it may be enjoyable hunting out bargains from junk stores, which could lead to some interesting finds, it can swallow up days without reward. How simple then, to open a mail-order catalogue, or walk into a department store, in the almost certain knowledge that you will find an item that suits your requirements. There is also, perhaps, the option of having something made to your exact specification. Another time-saving area is that spent on preparing your project prior to decoration. This can represent many hours saved on stripping, repairing, filling and sanding an item before the creative work can even begin (generally not most people's favourite aspect of decorating – and certainly not mine!).

In this book I've tried to include a wide range of decorative techniques to provide a good grounding in the basic skills required to enable the reader to tackle a variety of surfaces. The projects vary in style from faded grandeur to simple country and classic elegance. Giving them an aged appearance generally allows these new pieces to sit more comfortably alongside those already established in a room, and are appropriate for both traditional and more contemporary decorating schemes.

No particular drawing or painting skills are required to complete any of the projects in this book so I hope you will feel encouraged to have a go. Don't be too disheartened if you don't achieve the result you want at your first attempt. Experimenting, cleaning off and starting again are all part of the learning process. It does take a little practice to build up confidence with using colour, paint and glaze techniques and I do recommend practising on samples before embarking on a project. Offcuts of wood and medium-density fibreboard (MDF), or even pieces of card, can be painted, stencilled, varnished or waxed, as appropriate.

Manufacturers and suppliers seem to have been quick to respond to the growing number of decorating programmes on TV and the increased public interest in decorative products. There have been many new and mainly water-based paints, glazes and other products introduced to the retail sector to meet the needs of the DIY market. As a result, many materials that were once the preserve of the professional decorator or knowledgeable amateur can now be easily found in the large DIY stores and art and craft shops. There are a number of specialist decorating shops, listed at the end of the book, that will supply by mail order any products that you may have difficulty obtaining locally. So, get started, be creative, and I hope you enjoy yourself as much as I did putting this book together!

Basic techniques

*T*his chapter will provide you with all the information you need to prime and prepare your pieces for decoration, and covers a range of techniques that you will use to create your 'new antiques'. The materials and equipment that are required to complete the projects illustrated in this book are all carefully described and explained.

IS IT OIL-, WATER- OR SPIRIT- BASED?

This is a question that is frequently asked by those bewildered by the choice of paints available. In this book, you will be pleased to find out that, for the most part, water-based user-friendly products have been used. This means that water is used as the solvent and is also used for thinning and cleaning up. However, there are a number of exceptions so it is important to understand the basic make-up of all the paints and varnishes that you will be using.

You will generally find that decorating shops offer a choice of water- and oil-based paints and varnishes. Where possible, select water- rather than oil-based products; instructions in this book are usually given for these. It is not always immediately apparent as to which group a product belongs. For example, the term 'quick drying' is usually seen on a tin of acrylic varnish. However, it also appears on some oil-based tins. The solution is to read carefully the manufacturer's directions for cleaning brushes. If you are directed to use white spirit, you will know it is oil-based.

Spirit-based products require methylated spirit for cleaning. It is possible to buy cellulose-based paints and varnishes, but they are unpleasant to use and are not recommended.

TABLE OF WATER-, OIL-, AND SPIRIT-BASED PAINT PRODUCTS

	WATER BASED	OIL BASED	SPIRIT BASED
SOLVENT/THINNER	Water (methylated spirit on dry paint)	White spirit and turpentine	Methylated spirit
COLOURANT	Artist's acrylic paint, acrylic paint stains, universal paint stains, gouache, powder pigment	Artist's oil and alkyd paints, universal stainers, powder pigment	Spirit-based wood stains, spirit dyes
WOOD STAINS	Acrylic wood dye	White spirit soluble wood dye	Spirit wood dye
PRIMER/SEALER PAINT	Acrylic primers for wood, some metals, tiles and melamine	Metal, wood, tile and all-purpose oil primer	Shellac-based all-purpose primer for wood, metal, plaster, tiles, melamine
TOPCOAT PAINT	Vinyl silk and matt traditional paint	Flat, eggshell, satin oil paint	
ARTIST'S PAINT	Acrylic paint, gouache paint, watercolour paint	Oil paint, stencil paint sticks	
GLAZES	Acrylic scumble	Transparent oil glaze	
WAXES	Acrylic wax	Clear and coloured waxes, liquid wax	
CLEAR VARNISHES	Dead flat, matt, satin and gloss acrylic varnish	Dead flat, satin, acrylic and gloss polyurethane varnish	
SHELLAC			Shellac sanding sealer, knotting, transparent, white, button, french and garnet polish
ADHESIVES	PVA glue, paper paste, wallpaper paste, border adhesive		
GOLD SIZE	Acrylic gold size	Oil gold size	
GILT WAXES & VARNISHES	Metallic varnish	Gilt cream, gilt wax, gilt varnish	Mix bronzing powder with shellac to make varnish
CRACKLE GLAZE	Crackle glaze or gum arabic		
CRAQUELURE	Top coat cracking varnish of oil and water method, top and base coat of water-based method	Base coat ageing varnish of oil and water method	
LIMING	Liming paste	Liming wax	

PREPARATION

Most people enjoy painting, but not many like sanding, filling and laborious preparation. The big plus when decorating new furniture and effects is that minimal preparation, if any, is usually required, and you can get started straight away. The exception is highly lacquered surfaces which need to be well sanded to provide a key for the paint. An electric sander is a good investment for this task and it will also quickly smooth other surfaces before painting.

MATERIALS & EQUIPMENT

Acrylic primer can be used for wood, some metals, tiles and melamine. It is usually white in colour, easy to use and quick drying.

Oil-based primer is a slow-drying durable primer. It works well over metal and other smooth surfaces.

Shellac sanding sealer is used for sealing wood and papier mâché. Shellac is made from the naturally occurring resin of the lac beetle dissolved in methylated spirit to form a quick-drying varnish. It is a traditional product used for french polishing, woodstaining and sealing. Shellac comes in a variety of grades and colours, each of which have a different name (see the table on page 11 for more information).

PVA or acrylic varnish can be used to seal plaster before applying paint.

Sandpaper comes in a range from fine to coarse. Fine- to medium-grade sandpaper is used to smooth a surface before painting. Medium- to coarse-grade sandpaper is used to roughen a smooth surface to provide a key for the paint. A sanding block is useful for wrapping the papers round when working on a flat surface as this makes sanding easier.

Wire wool also ranges from very fine to coarse. Fine 00-grade wire wool dipped in white spirit is used for removing wax.

Electric sanders make light work of smoothing wood surfaces and removing unwanted paint and varnish. The one pictured on the right has a pointed end that reaches easily into tricky corners that would otherwise be hard to rub down.

Wood filler is used for filling holes and cracks in wooden surfaces. There are many types available, including water-based varieties. Follow the manufacturer's instructions for use.

SURFACES

Most surfaces are suitable for decoration but often they will need to be coated with an appropriate primer first to seal the surface and to enable the paint to adhere. Water-based primers are now available for a variety of applications and they are generally very effective. Make sure you use the correct primer for your particular surface, and follow the manufacturer's instructions carefully.

New wood You should normally seal new wood with either clear shellac sanding sealer or an acrylic wood primer. Shellac dries clear, so choose this if you are distressing layers of paint and revealing the wood beneath. Acrylic primer is pleasanter to use, so if you are going to use a technique where the primer will not be visible, it would be a good choice. Start by filling any holes or cracks with wood filler, then sand the surface using a fine- to medium-grade sandpaper. Next, brush on the shellac or acrylic wood primer and leave to dry. If you have used acrylic primer, you will need to sand the surface smooth again, before painting.

New painted, varnished or polished wood It is best to choose a finish that will cover an unsuitable paint colour. It is usually only necessary to rub the article down with a fine- to coarse-grade sandpaper, to roughen the surface a little, so that the paint applied over will adhere. If necessary, you can brush shellac or acrylic primer on before painting.

Varnished surfaces will need a considerable amount of sanding before painting and an electric sander is particularly useful here.

Polish should be thoroughly removed from wood, or paint applied over it will not adhere. Use 00-grade wire wool dipped in white spirit to remove the polish, then sand with a medium-grade sandpaper when it is dry.

Medium density fibreboard (MDF) Good quality flat MDF needs no preparation before applying paint. Occasionally, you may find a poorer quality MDF with an absorbent surface, where the paint practically disappears by the time it has dried. In this case, prime the MDF as for new wood, or seal with acrylic varnish. Machine-moulded edges on MDF can roughen with painting and benefit from being sealed to provide a smoother painted surface.

Metal Raw metal should be primed with a suitable primer, according to type, following the manufacturer's instructions. This is to prevent rust forming on the metal. Painted metal is treated in the same way as painted wood.

Enamel Prime new enamel with an oil-based metal primer or a water-based tile primer.

Papier mâché Seal papier mâché by brushing on a coat of shellac sanding sealer. This will prevent the paint being absorbed in the surface.

Terracotta Unglazed terracotta needs no special treatment and can be painted directly with paint. Lightly glazed terracotta should be rubbed down with coarse-grade sandpaper before painting to provide a roughened surface for the paint to adhere. A highly glazed terracotta surface will need priming with a tile primer.

Plastic Plastic can be primed with acrylic melamine primer, shellac primer or shellac. If the surface is shiny and smooth, paint will not adhere well, so rub it down first with medium-grade sandpaper to roughen the surface and improve the adhesion of a primer.

Plaster Plaster can be sealed by brushing on PVA, acrylic varnish, shellac or shellac primer. This will prevent paint from being absorbed in the surface of the plaster.

AGEING WOOD AND METAL

There are ways to treat new wood and metal surfaces in order to give a more realistic aged appearance to your finished project. Wood can be bashed about, stained and even burnt, depending on the style of decoration you choose and degree of ageing you require. Metal projects can benefit from being given a rusting metal paint effect applied as a base colour or even used on its own on hinges and other fittings.

WOOD

Taking away the brand new appearance of wood is important if you want to age a new piece of furniture realistically and there are several ways in which to achieve this. A combination of bashing and staining is effective in giving the impression of time-worn age, while torching wood can make it look really ancient.

Bashing

Staining

Burning

Bashing Newly planed smooth timber and crisp edges will need attacking and you will simply have to overcome any feeling that you are being destructive or ruining a perfectly good piece of furniture. Collect together various tools to mount your assault. A hammer is essential, together with screwdrivers, bradawls, nails and chisels. Use these to dent, scrape, chip and scratch the surface. Sharp edges can be sanded with coarse-grade sandpaper to round them, or flattened with a hammer. Nails can be used to scratch the surface and create worm holes.

Staining Wood can be darkened by brushing it with either brown shellac or wood dye. Staining with shellac has the advantage of also sealing the wood, but the choice of available colours is narrow. Garnet polish is the darkest shellac, but it is a bit too orange to resemble old wood; add the tiniest amount of green spirit dye to tone down the colour.

Acrylic dyes are available in a large number of wood and other shades and, being solvent free, they are pleasanter to use. A mix of 1 part dark oak to 2 parts antique pine stain produces a good 'old timber' colour. The amount of colour absorbed by a piece of wood varies so it is a good idea to dilute the colour with 2 or 3 parts water. This allows you to darken the colour with another layer if you need to, and avoids the problem of the stain being too dark and difficult to remove. If you want a sealed surface, brush shellac sanding sealer over the surface.

Burning Burning new wood with a blow torch is the most aggressive ageing technique as it literally removes most of the top surface, leaving a hard raised grain. You will need to scorch the wood by holding the flame against the surface, until it looks quite black. A stiff wire brush is then scrubbed over the burnt wood to remove the charred surface. The wood can then be limed or painted.

METAL

Several of the metal projects in this book have been painted with a base coat to give the appearance of rusting metal. In most cases, the metal already had a black coating, but if not, or if the surface is very smooth and new looking, you can paint it with two coats of black emulsion paint. Apply the paint with a sponge paint roller to avoid brushmarks and give the surface a pitted texture, rather like hammered metal. Two shades of brown and rust-coloured emulsion paint are used to create the rust effect. If you like, you can omit step 2, using the mid-brown shade, especially if not much of the rust effect will be visible beneath the topcoat.

Steps 4 and 5 complete the technique, and give a realistic look of old rusting metal; this looks good on metal fittings or other items where this effect is the only one used. These steps are not necessary if you plan to paint over the rust.

YOU WILL NEED

Stencil brush

Emulsion paint: dark brown, medium brown and rust

Paper towels

Sponge paint roller

Matt acrylic varnish

Rag

Rottenstone powder

1 Dip a stencil brush into dark brown emulsion paint. Dab the brush a few times on a paper towel to remove the excess paint, then stipple the colour randomly over the black base coat. Leave to dry.

2 Stipple medium brown emulsion paint sparingly over the dark brown colour as in step 1. Apply more paint to some areas than others, to give a random mottled effect.

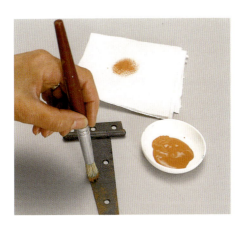

3 When dry, stipple on the rust-coloured paint sparingly here and there over the surface, placing most of the colour around the edges where rust would naturally occur. Allow to dry.

4 Using a sponge paint roller, apply matt acrylic varnish over the hinges; this will avoid leaving brushmarks. Leave the varnish for about ten minutes so that it becomes clear and feels just dry.

5 Dip a dry rag into some rottenstone powder and rub this gently over the varnished surface. The varnish should be just tacky enough at this stage that a small amount of the rottenstone will adhere to it and give a dirty appearance to the finish. Allow to dry.

PAINTING AND AGEING PAINT

Water-based paint has been used for all the painted projects in this book. This is more or less odour-free, quicker drying and easier to use than oil paint. Paint now comes in such a good range of designer palettes, ranging from muted Victorian and Georgian shades to bright Caribbean and Mediterranean ones, that there hardly ever seems the need to mix your own. However, should you want to change your paint colour, you can add acrylic paint and stains, universal stains or powdered pigment. Tester and sample pots are usually available, and these are a very economical way of decorating small items.

You can choose from standard emulsion paint or from one of the traditional paint ranges now available. Traditional paints have a chalky-based texture and are based on natural rather than synthetic pigments. This type of paint is quite soft and easily marked, and touching-in a spoilt area often leaves a watermark. This is not a problem with distressed effects, but it may be if you want a perfect painted surface. You can mix emulsion paint together with traditional paint and both can be diluted with water to make colourwashes, or added to scumble to make glazes. There are numerous ways of giving paint an aged appearance. You will find that each project in Chapter 1 uses a completely different technique.

PAINT

Emulsion paint comes in an enormous range of colours and a choice of a matt or satin finish. It is a tough plastic paint that is waterproof when dry; paint should not be allowed to dry on brushes. The paint is usually dry in less than an hour, but recoating time is normally two hours. Traditional paint is usually made from natural rather than synthetic pigments and it contains chalk and other traditional paint-making ingredients. The paint dries to a matt finish in half an hour when it can then be overpainted. The chalky texture makes traditional paint very absorbent and also appears considerably lighter when dry. Applying varnish and wax to seal will darken the colour. The paint is not skin-forming and handles very well when creating a distressed finish.

Acrylic paint is quick drying, durable and very versatile. Its concentrated colour makes it ideal for mixing with paints and glazes. It is also used for surface decoration, including stencilling and hand painting. Acrylic colour is waterproof when dry, and brushes must be washed in water immediately after use. Acrylic colour is

available in tubes and jars and in thick and more fluid consistencies.

Gouache paint is opaque matt paint and can be found in similar colours to acrylic paint. The main practical difference between the two is that gouache is water soluble, making it unsuitable for many applications, such as stencilling.

Paint stains, either acrylic or universal, are highly concentrated liquid pigment which can be aded to paints, varnishes and glazes to colour them. They are available in a limited number of colours but these can easily be mixed to provide a wide range of different shades.

Powdered pigments are natural earth and mineral pigments in powder form which can be mixed with paints, varnishes, acrylic mediums and wax. They are available in a wonderful range of colours from most good art and specialist decorating shops.

GLAZES AND MEDIUMS

Acrylic scumble glaze is a slow-drying water-based transparent medium. It has a gel-like consistency which enables it to hold the marks made by brushes, sponges and other tools. You can mix approximately 1 part emulsion/traditional paint to 6 parts scumble to make a translucent glaze.

Alternatively, you can make a more transparent colour by adding acrylic paint, gouache, paint stains or powder pigment to the glaze. Add sufficient colour until you have reached the intensity that you require. Drying times vary according to make and you will need to follow the individual manufacturer's advice.

Acrylic medium is water based and white in appearance, but it dries clear. It can be mixed with acrylic, gouache, universal stainers or powder pigment to make thin paints and washes. It is available in matt or gloss finishes and is quick drying. Acrylic retarder can be added to the medium to slow the drying time.

Vinegar medium is a traditional medium much used in early folk painting. It is made by adding sugar to vinegar, then powdered pigment is added to this. Vinegar medium is water soluble and should be fixed with shellac or oil varnish. Spray varnishes can also be used.

Crackle glaze is a water-soluble glaze that is applied as a sandwich between two layers of paint or between wood and paint. It usually dries clear in about half an hour, and causes the paint that is applied over the dry glaze to crack. This gives the appearance of peeling paint. Individual brands may vary; follow each manufacturer's advice accordingly.

PAINTING EQUIPMENT

Paintbrushes in a variety of widths are needed for applying paint. The most useful sizes for painting the projects in this book are 1.5cm (0 in), 2.5cm (1in) and 4cm (10 in). You can use either household paintbrushes, thinner flat varnish brushes, or hog fitches, whichever you prefer.

Paint rollers are available in mini sizes with different textures. The sponge and smooth textures are very good for applications where brushmarks would spoil the effect.

Badger softeners are very soft, long-haired brushes that are gently brushed over thin wet paint or glaze, to smooth away brushmarks from the surface.

Sea sponges are used to apply paints and glazes to give a subtle textured effect. Alternatively, they can be applied damp over wet paint and glaze to remove paint and texture the surface.

Stockinette is used for dabbing over wet paint to blend, texture, soften or absorb paint. It is also useful for mopping up any paint spills.

Masking tape is available in various widths and types and keeps paint within a confined area. Choose low-tack masking tape for sticking over paintwork, and plastic-backed tape for easing around curved surfaces.

DISTRESSING EQUIPMENT AND ABRASIVES

Sandpaper in fine and medium grades is used to distress paint and to smooth between layers, if necessary.

Silicone carbide finishing paper can be found in the same grades as sandpaper as well as in much finer grades, and it is also used for distressing and smoothing. Finishing paper is gentler than sandpaper and less likely to scratch a painted surface.

Wire wool and methylated spirit Very fine 0000-grade wire wool dipped in methylated spirit is used for gently rubbing back paint.

A blow torch provides a quick method of removing paint and achieving a heavily distressed appearance.

Clear liquid wax is used as a resist for paint. It is applied with a small brush over areas of a surface where you want the paintwork to look worn.

Latex or art masking fluid is also used as a paint resist and is applied with a small brush in the same way as liquid wax. It has the effect of making paintwork look chipped. Brushes should be washed immediately in water, but can be dipped in dry-cleaning fluid to remove latex and art masking fluid if they become solid.

Sand and shellac Sand is sprinkled over tacky shellac so that it sticks and forms a resist to paint applied over it.

PLANNING AND APPLYING A DESIGN

You will need to choose if you are going to add a decorative design to your project or leave it simple. You should consider where the piece is to be placed and look at other items you may have in the room before you finally decide what would be appropriate. None of the techniques described in this book are difficult and all are suitable for the inexperienced. However, some people new to decorative painting feel stencilling is the least inhibiting technique to start with.

MATERIALS & EQUIPMENT

Tracing and transfer paper Tracing paper is required for tracing designs from the template pages at the end of this book. Transfer paper or graphite paper is available in a choice of colours and it has a chalky surface. It is placed between the traced design and the surface to be decorated. The image is then transferred by drawing over with either a pencil or ballpoint pen without ink.

Drawing equipment A pencil, rubber and ruler are required for measuring and marking out designs. Chinagraph or water-soluble pencil marks are more easily removed. A centring ruler, available from graphic art suppliers, is a very useful piece of equipment.

Painting equipment Fine artist's paintbrushes are used for painting designs using various mediums.

Stencil film is a polyester film used for making stencils. It can be either shiny on both sides, or with a matt surface on one side, which is the kind used here. Trace the design onto the matt surface with a pencil then cut it out to make the stencil. If you cannot find matt-surfaced film, you will need a pen to trace your design. Alternatively, you can use a sheet of thick acetate and trace the design with a pen suitable for drawing on acetate.

Cutting equipment A scalpel knife and cutting mat are required for stencil cutting and découpage. A pair of sharp manicure scissors is also required for découpage. A heat-pen can be used instead of a scalpel for cutting either stencil film or acetate stencils. You simply trace over the design with the hot nib, and this melts the film and cuts out the stencil. You will need a sheet of thick glass to protect your working surface.

Stencil brushes and paint rollers Stencil brushes are round firm-bristled brushes used for applying paint through a stencil. They can also be used for stippling paint on to a surface. Using small foam rollers is a very quick and easy way of applying paint through a stencil when only a single colour is used.

Masking tape is needed to hold traced designs in place and to keep paint within a confined area and for creating borders and lines. Very narrow 'fine line tape' or car striping tape is good for painting narrow lines. Look out for low-tack tapes to prevent paint being lifted from the surface when removing tape.

Adhesives PVA, paper paste or wallpaper adhesives are required for découpage and other projects using paper sheets. Repositional spray adhesive is required to stick découpage designs temporarily in place before gluing, and to hold stencils in position so that paint does not seep under the edges.

PLANNING A DESIGN

Although there are patterns printed at the end of the book, you may wish to find your own. There are many books of copyright-free designs that are published for use by artists and craftspeople and you will find an address for these in the suppliers section on page 140. These include stencil designs and other designs suitable for découpage or transferring and handpainting. A wide range of styles is available and many of these are taken from historic sources.

Positioning a design When you have chosen a design, you will need to marry it with a project of suitable proportions. The easiest way to enlarge or reduce a design to fit is by using a photocopier. Concentrate on the main pattern of the design to start with, then use coloured borders, lines or individual motifs to fill gaps or enhance a design where appropriate.

Whether stencilling, handpainting or using découpage, it is important that you position a design accurately and you should use a chinagraph or other pencil and a ruler for measuring and marking out. You will usually need to find the centre of a flat surface and place the design on each side of this, starting from the middle and working outwards. A centring ruler is very useful for accurate marking for these purposes, saving the need for any mathematical calculations.

Placing a design on a round surface is slightly trickier as you need to ensure a continuous design that can be viewed from any angle. You will need to measure the object you want to decorate, using string or a tape measure, and work out roughly how many repeats of the design will fit into the measurement. You can then work out an exact measurement by dividing this number into the measurement of the circumference and then scaling the design up or down, as appropriate, using a

photocopier. For example, a design with a 6cm (2½ in) repeat will fit roughly five times around a box with a 32cm (11in) circumference. For the design to fit exactly it will need to measure 6.4cm (2⅝ in).

To enlarge or reduce a design to fit, use a calculator to divide the size you want by the size you have and multiply by 100; for example, here it would be 6.4 ÷ 6 = 1.06 x 100 = 106% enlargement.

TRANSFERRING AND PAINTING A DESIGN

In transferring a design, you do not need any special drawing or painting skills to achieve professional looking results. Simply trace and transfer a design, then fill in the outline with a single colour. Finer details can be overlaid by transferring them over the blocked colour and drawing or painting over the marks, as appropriate. You can use either a pencil or a ballpoint pen without ink to transfer the design. However, if the design is going to be repeated several times, it is better to use a ballpoint pen, so that your traced drawing remains crisp and clean.

YOU WILL NEED

Template

Tracing paper

Pencil

Ruler

Masking tape

Transfer paper

Ballpoint pen without ink (optional)

Fine pointed artist's paintbrush

Acrylic paint or other medium

Fine finishing paper (optional)

1 Trace the design from the template using tracing paper and a pencil.

2 Use a pencil and ruler to mark the position of the design. Secure two sides of the traced design in position with masking tape. Slide a piece of transfer paper beneath the tracing and secure with more tape if it is necessary.

3 Transfer the design by going over the outlines of the image with a ballpoint pen. Check that all the design has been transferred before moving the tracing.

4 Fill in the design as neatly as you can using a fine pointed paintbrush and acrylic paint. Edges can be softened with fine finishing paper if you like.

STENCILLING

Stencilling is a wonderfully quick way of applying a design. There is a huge range of excellent ready-made stencils available but it is quite simple and more economical to make your own. You can use many different types of paint for stencilling and not just those sold for the purpose. Acrylic paints are very versatile and can be used for both striking and subtle effects. Oil stencil sticks are very easy to use and give a light layer of soft colour. The most important rule when stencilling is not to put too much paint on the brush. Thick gunky paint looks unattractive and is likely to seep under the stencil, creating untidy edges. Attaching the stencil to the surface with repositional spray adhesive helps to contain the paint within the stencilled area. Keep plenty of paper towels handy for dabbing off the excess paint on your stencil brushes.

MAKING A STENCIL

YOU WILL NEED

Template

*Stencil film and pencil or
acetate and pen for drawing on acetate*

*Scalpel and cutting mat or
heat-pen and glass*

1 Trace the design directly on to stencil film with a pencil or on to acetate with a pen.

2 *Cutting with scalpel.* Place the design over a cutting mat or a piece of thick card and carefully cut around the design with the point of the scalpel knife. If your scalpel overruns and you cut into a bridge (a little connecting strip that holds the stencil together) you can mend it with a small strip of masking tape.

3 *Cutting with heat-pen.* Place the design over a piece of thick glass and, when the pen is hot, draw over the stencil film with the hot nib. You need to apply gentle, even pressure and cut at a steady rate. Too much pressure will not speed the process; it will merely result in untidy edges, and may cause the nib to bend.

DECOUPAGE

Découpage is a brilliant way of using ready-painted designs either to give the illusion that your work has been handpainted, or simply as a means of adding design and ornament. The process involves cutting out a printed image, such as flowers or other motifs from a piece of giftwrap, and gluing them to a surface. Usually several coats of varnish are applied over the image so that it becomes integral to the surface.

All paper should be sealed on the printed side with a coat of clear shellac before cutting out the motif. This will make the paper stronger and less likely to tear, and protect the printed surface from any damage that may otherwise occur during the gluing process.

You will need to have a really sharp pair of scissors and a scalpel knife for cutting out designs. First, cut out any internal areas of the design with a scalpel knife pressed firmly over the paper, then use scissors to cut around the edges.

Arrange the cut-out design on your object, using repositional spray adhesive to hold the pieces of paper in place. When you are happy with your arrangement, glue the design in place and smooth out all bubbles of air from the centre of the paper towards to the edges. Wash off excess glue with a damp sponge and leave it to dry for two hours or more. You can use either PVA or paste glue. Paste glue is easier as it does not dry so quickly, leaving more time to make minor adjustments and smooth the surface. When dry, use a pencil, if necessary, to touch in any visible white edges of paper.

You will need to apply between three and ten coats of satin acrylic varnish over the découpaged design, depending on the finish that you require. Leave at least two hours' drying time between each coat and sand between layers if you like. You can change to matt varnish for the final two coats, if you prefer a matt finish.

GILDING

The gilding techniques used in this book are not difficult to master. There are two basic methods used – gilding over water-based size and gilding over oil-based size. Bronzing powder or metal leaf can be used with either sort of gold size and they are applied when the size has reached the right level of tack or stickiness. Gilding with acrylic size is the simplest method, as the drying time for the gold size is not critical and you can start the gilding process 15 or 20 minutes after you have applied the size. The gold size used for the oil-gilded projects in this book takes two to four hours to reach the right tack.

MATERIALS & EQUIPMENT

Metal leaf comes in packs of 25 squares and is available in loose or transfer form. Transfer leaf has a waxed paper backing for transferring it to a surface. Each sheet consists of finely beaten metal: imitation gold, aluminium and copper leaf are used for the projects in this book. These are much less expensive than real gold and silver and very effective when used for decorative techniques.

Bronzing powders are finely ground metallic powders made from bronze, aluminium and copper. They are dusted on to a tacky size and look less shiny than metal leaf, but have more lustre than metallic paint. Bronze powder can also be mixed with acrylic mediums, varnish and shellac to make a gold paint.

Acrylic gold size is a water-based size to which the metal leaf adheres. It has a milky appearance when brushed on the surface but becomes transparent very quickly. The size is ready to gild over in about 15 minutes, but it stays tacky indefinitely, so you can leave it longer if you like. Large areas will need to be worked fairly quickly, because if you over-brush an area that has started to dry, you will disturb the surface and it will become lumpy.

Gold oil size is a slower drying size rather like an oil-based varnish. It is free-flowing and self-levelling which means that it dries without brushmarks. This provides a smoother surface for the metal and a better quality to the finish. Oil size is available with different drying times to reach the right tack for gilding, for example 3-hour, 12-hour and 24-hour. A basic gold size available from decorating shops takes two to four hours and Japan gold size is usually dry in one to two hours.

Soft flat synthetic brushes are best for applying acrylic size so that brushmarks are kept to a minimum. Brushmarks will show beneath the thin leaf and may spoil the appearance. The same brushes can also be used for oil-based size, ensuring a thin even application.

Soft round brushes are used for dusting the bronzing powder over tacky size. They can also be used for dusting off excess bronzing powder.

Scissors are required for cutting the loose and transfer leaf into strips.

FINISHING

You may need to finish your project with varnish and/or wax to provide a durable surface or pleasing finish. Choose varnish for kitchens and bathrooms, where wax would not be appropriate, and for other projects where you require a durable finish. Apart from découpage projects, two or three coats should be sufficient. If you require a flat smooth surface, use a fine-grade finishing paper or sandpaper over the varnished surface before applying the final layer or two of varnish. You can apply wax over varnish, but the varnish will need to be matt, as wax does not adhere well to a slippery surface. Wax can be applied directly over paint or varnish. Coloured waxes will be more staining over paint than varnish, which is less absorbent.

MATERIALS & EQUIPMENT

Acrylic varnish is water based and available in gloss, satin, matt and dead flat finishes. The varnish is milky in appearance, but dries to a clear finish and is non-yellowing. Acrylic varnishes are usually touch dry in about 20 minutes and recoatable after two hours. Clean brushes immediately after use with water.

Oil-based varnish is available in gloss, satin, matt and dead flat finishes and is slow drying. It is usually recoatable after about eight hours or the following day and, although it is generally more durable and heat-proof than water-based varnish, it does yellow with time. Work in a well-ventilated room and clean brushes with white spirit.

Two-part crackle varnishes are available in oil and water, or water-based only formulas. The oil and water technique involves a quick-drying water-soluble varnish being placed over a just tacky, slow-drying oil-based varnish. There are several two-part water-based craquelure products on the market, and you will need to follow the individual manufacturer's advice for directions of use. In both cases, the cracking occurs once the second coat of varnish has dried.

Raw umber oil paint is rubbed into a cracked surface and left to dry overnight. This makes the cracks more visible, adding to the aged look.

Clear wax can be used over paint and varnish to give a soft sheen without changing the colour. Rottenstone can be added to make a dirty coloured wax.

Brown or antiquing furniture waxes are staining and are a quick way of adding age. Walnut and oak shades are good for ageing all colours of paint. Antiquing and pine-coloured waxes are generally yellowing and therefore should be avoided on blue.

Liming wax is white in colour and can be used to give a white bloom to paint in addition to giving a limed finish to wood.

Gilt creams are a mix of finely ground metal powder and wax. They are good for adding a touch of glitter over paint or varnish. A wide choice of colours is available and they can be applied with either a brush or finger. When the cream is dry, buff with a soft cloth and seal with clear shellac for a more durable finish.

Varnish brushes Flat varnish brushes are particularly good for applying varnish, but you can use an ordinary household paintbrush if you prefer.

Soft cloths and 0000-grade wire wool are used for applying and buffing wax.

CHAPTER 1

Peeling back the layers

*T*here are many ways to achieve
a peeled and worn surface
giving painted furniture a lived-in
appearance, suitable for traditional
and contemporary homes.
Most of these are quick and simple.

ROCOCO FRAME

A carved surface is perfect for distressing as the raised areas will be worn more than the recessed areas, producing a lovely decorative effect. Pale creamy layers of paint are applied over this rococo-style frame, then the raised relief is simply rubbed with fine wire wool and methylated spirit to reveal the dark wood beneath.

YOU WILL NEED

Carved wooden frame

0000-grade wire wool

White spirit

Two shades of cream emulsion/traditional paint

5cm (2in) paintbrush

Methylated spirit

This is a very simple project because you don't have to decide which areas would look best rubbed back. By gently rubbing the frame with wire wool soaked in methylated spirit, you will automatically remove paint from the raised areas of carving, which in fact replicates the way this type of frame would naturally wear. If you remove too much paint, simply re-apply some more. The use of pale paint lightens the heavy appearance of the dark wood and two close shades of colour can provide a subtle texture. However, this technique works perfectly well when only a single colour is used.

1 Remove any wax from the frame with wire wool dipped in white spirit. Paint the frame with dark cream paint and leave to dry.

2 Apply a lighter shade of cream paint over the entire frame, and leave to dry again.

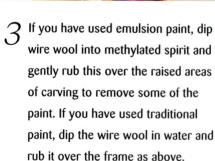

3 If you have used emulsion paint, dip wire wool into methylated spirit and gently rub this over the raised areas of carving to remove some of the paint. If you have used traditional paint, dip the wire wool in water and rub it over the frame as above.

ROMAN POTS

Natural earth colours of pale terracotta, red and yellow ochre are dry-brushed with off-white paint over the surface of these rustic terracotta pots to create an aged look. The wet paint is then distressed with a damp sponge to give the pots a timeless appeal.

YOU WILL NEED

Terracotta pot

Earth-coloured shades of emulsion/traditional paint

5cm (2in) paintbrush

Off-white emulsion/traditional paint

Household sponge

Dry-brushing is the term used to describe painting with only a small amount of paint on the end of the bristles, so that they are almost dry. The surfaces of the pots are uneven and lumpy and the randomly applied and blended top coat gives the appearance of age-worn paint. Because the pots are hand-thrown, horizontal ridges are apparent on the surface. The paint should be brushed around the pot following these circular markings. If you are using emulsion paint and working on a large pot, you will need to wipe off the paint fairly quickly before it becomes too dry to remove. Traditional paint is the easier and preferable option, as you can remove it by rubbing a bit more vigorously with a damp sponge, even after the paint has dried.

1 Paint inside the rim of the pot then over the outside with your chosen paint colour. When dry, apply a second coat if required. Allow to dry.

2 Dip a brush into a small amount of off-white paint and brush it sparingly around the pot, allowing patches of the base coat to show through.

3 Before the paint has dried, wipe a damp sponge around the pot to blend and remove some of the paint. Allow to dry.

SHAKER PEG RAIL

The surface of the wood on this pine rail has been artificially worn by burning it with a blow torch and scrubbing away the burnt wood, leaving a raised grain. The resulting driftwood appearance is achieved by brushing a coat of liming paste over the entire surface.

YOU WILL NEED

Wooden peg rail
Blow torch
Wire brush
Liming paste
5cm (2in) paintbrush
00-grade wire wool
Matt or satin acrylic varnish
Varnish brush

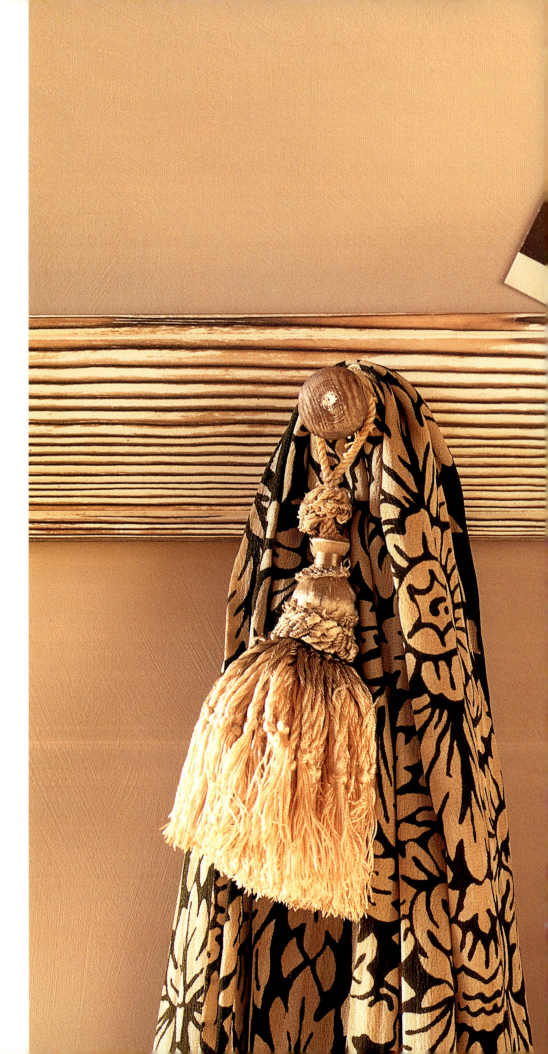

This is a very simple and effective way of achieving a worn look on new pine. The blow torch should be used to burn the surface until it looks black; when this surface is then brushed with a wire brush, it will appear noticeably ridged. When using the blow torch, care must be taken to protect surrounding areas from risk of fire.

A limed finish has been given to this project, but you can use this technique to age and give depth to flat wooden surfaces before applying a distressed paint effect.

If you prefer, you can use liming wax instead of paste over the torched wood, but the whitening effect will be less pronounced. If using wax, apply it with 0000-grade wire wool and leave it on for about half an hour before rubbing off the excess with another pad of wire wool. Do not apply acrylic varnish over the waxed finish.

3 Brush a generous coat of liming paste over the entire peg rail and leave it to dry.

1 Scorch the surface of the wood using a blow torch, holding it so that the flame is against the surface, until the wood turns black.

2 Scrub the surface of the peg rail with a wire brush to remove all the charred wood; this will make the surface look ridged.

4 Remove the excess paste by rubbing the surface with wire wool, so that it is lifted off the raised grain but remains in the deep ridges of the wood. Seal the surface with a coat of matt or satin acrylic varnish.

Liming wax has been used on the top peg rail (left). This has a more subtle effect than liming paste. The bottom peg rail was first painted with dilute dark blue paint, then liming paste was applied over the top.

INDIAN CUPBOARD

Wax resist and a heatgun are the simple tricks behind the heavily worn appearance of the paint on this Indian cupboard. The jewel-bright colours of lime green and blue liven up an otherwise sombre cupboard and are entirely in keeping with its exotic origins.

YOU WILL NEED

Wooden cupboard

00- and 0000-grade wire wool

White spirit

Masking tape

Artist's brush

Clear liquid wax

Emulsion/traditional paint: lime green, emerald green and turquoise

2.5cm (1in) paintbrush

Heatgun

Scraper

Soft cloth

This cupboard may look old, but it is typical of the style of new hardwood pieces of furniture that are being exported from India today and can be found in many furniture stores. The furniture is usually coated with a dark staining wax, which has to be removed before painting. Paint will not adhere to a surface where there is wax and although the odd patch may not matter, most of the paint will need to stick.

The bright lime green paint used here would probably be hard to live with on its own, but the colour works well beneath the darker, slightly softer, blue and green shades. It is a good idea to mask off any fittings that are not removable before painting, as this is much quicker than carefully going around them with a fine brush or cleaning off smudges later.

Clear liquid wax is easier to apply with a brush than solid wax, but either can be used. The wax is brushed on to areas of natural wear, such as the door edges and other random places. A wax candle can be used as an alternative to clear wax, but the result tends to be more streaky, and less controllable. The wax acts as a resist for the paint and will be melted with a heatgun once the paint on top has dried. A heatgun is not strictly necessary but it makes light work of giving this cupboard a very heavily distressed appearance.

The paint over the melted wax is removed by scraping and then by going over the surface with wire wool. Sometimes more of the paint than you would like is removed, but this is simple to rectify by touching up with more paint and rubbing back with wire wool to blend. You don't need to worry about re-waxing in this case.

1 Dip 0000-grade wire wool in white spirit and rub this over the cupboard to remove surface wax. Cover all the metal fittings on the cupboard with strips of masking tape to prevent paint being splashed on to them.

6 Taking care to protect surrounding surfaces, hold a heatgun close to the painted surface until the wax melts and the paint starts to bubble. Repeat over all the waxed areas.

4 Repeat the application of liquid wax over the lime green paint as in step 2. Leave to dry for 30 minutes.

2 Using an artist's brush, apply liquid wax to the edges and other external surfaces of the cupboard where you want the paint to appear chipped. Work quickly and roll the brush as you go for a more random and pleasing appearance. Leave the wax to dry for at least half an hour.

7 Using a scraper and 00-grade wire wool, gently remove the bubbled paint from the surface. Touch up any areas of paintwork where you feel it is necessary. Complete the cupboard by applying clear wax over the paintwork and buffing to a shine with a soft cloth. This will protect the paint and nourish the wood.

3 Paint over all the waxed surfaces with a coat of lime green paint and leave to dry thoroughly.

5 Brush emerald green paint over the lime green base coat in the areas of your choice. When dry, repeat with the turquoise colour. Allow to dry.

VICTORIAN PLANTER

This Victorian-inspired planter has been given a decorative rusting metal treatment. Sand was the unusual ingredient used as a resist to give the appearance of paint pitted by the corrosion of the metal beneath. The sand needs to be scraped away once the paint has been applied: a wooden spatula or lollipop stick is ideal for doing this. A knife or other sharp instrument will scratch off too much of the paint.

YOU WILL NEED

Wirework planter

Stencil brush

Brown/rust shades of emulsion paint (see page 15)

Clear shellac

Small paintbrush

Sand

Small tray

Duck-egg blue emulsion paint

Wooden spatula or lollipop stick

This prettily shaped wire planter was bought from a garden centre. Standing at 1m (40in) high, it was quite an ambitious project, not that decorating wirework is difficult, but it is laborious because of its intricacy. Decorating this wire planter took six stages to achieve the effect, but it was worth it as the finished result looks just like old and rusting painted wirework. No other resist is nearly as effective. To achieve this effect, shellac is brushed over a rust paint finish and then sand is sprinkled on to the wet shellac which acts like an adhesive for the grains. Only a small area at a time can be worked on as shellac dries quickly; when it is dry the sand will not adhere. If the shellac does dry before you have sprinkled on all the sand, don't worry – simply paint more shellac over the top.

A top coat of emulsion paint is applied over the shellac and sand. Here a pretty duck-egg blue has been used but you will often see antique wire planters painted white, so choose this colour if you want a more traditional look that will fit with any colour scheme.

1 Using a stencil brush, stipple two or three shades of brown/rust paint on all sides of the planter, following the instructions on page 15.

2 Brush some shellac on to a small area of the planter.

3 Immediately, sprinkle the wet surface with sand. Hold the tray containing sand beneath your working area so that surplus grains can fall into the tray. Continue to apply shellac and sprinkle sand over the entire planter.

4 When the planter is dry, paint it with a coat of duck-egg blue emulsion and leave to dry again.

5 Using a wooden spatula, scrape off the grains of sand to reveal the rust colour beneath. It is not necessary to remove all the sand as the lumpy paint surface simply adds to the decorative effect.

RUSTIC CUPBOARD

A brand new piece of pine furniture can be made to look a hundred years old in just a day. Although the process of authentically replicating a naturally aged piece is many layered, each layer is quick and easy to do.

YOU WILL NEED

Pine bathroom cupboard

Fine- and medium-grade sandpaper

Sanding block

Dark oak and antique pine water-based wood dye

5cm (2in) paintbrush

Art masking fluid

Fine hog brush

Watercolour brush

Emulsion/traditional paint: beige, old white, black, dark brown and rust

Tools for bashing: screwdriver, hammer, chisel and scraper

00- and 0000-grade wire wool

Household sponge

Small paint roller and tray

Cotton rag

Rottenstone

Woodstain

Matt acrylic varnish

Varnish brush

This cupboard is made from new pine so taking away the clean appearance of the wood is the first step in creating a realistic aged effect. Art masking fluid is used as a resist to leave some areas of the cupboard without paint. In order to make the aged and worn appearance of the paint look authentic, you need to pay attention to those areas of natural wear, for example, the part of the door that would be worn by continually turning the wooden catch, the door knob that would have little paint remaining after constant handling, and the feet that are likely to have been subjected to a good deal of foot scuffing. The cupboard is bashed and battered after each layer of paint is applied, because this imitates the natural sequence of events. To make it easier to decorate the cupboard door, remove the hinges first. These can then be given an antique treatment and painted to look like hammered metal with a hint of rust.

The paint that is used for the project is a traditional chalky-based one and this is simply finished by buffing with fine wire wool so that it looks like old milk paint. The cupboard will then continue to age naturally. If you want to halt this ageing process and have a more practical bathroom cupboard, finish with two coats of matt acrylic varnish. This is, in any case, recommended for the unpainted top surface for greater durability.

1 Remove the hinges and fittings from the cupboard and smooth all the surfaces with fine-grade sandpaper wrapped around a sanding block.

2 Apply water-based wood dye following the instructions on page 14 for the ageing wood technique.

3 Using a fine hog brush, dab art masking fluid here and there in the middle of the panels of wood, then apply it more liberally to the edges.

Vary the marks by dabbing, dragging and rolling the brush for different effects. Try to work quickly for a free and random appearance.

4 Dip a brush into the masking fluid and spatter this over the surface by tapping the handle with a second brush. Vary the amount of spattering in different areas for a more realistic appearance. Leave the masking fluid to become clear and dry.

5 Brush a coat of beige paint over the masked surface in the direction of the wood grain, and leave to dry. It does not matter if this is applied unevenly as a patchy effect will add to the distressed appearance.

7 Repeat the paint resist technique with masking fluid, as in steps 3 and 4, then brush on a coat of old white paint and leave to dry.

10 Rub the hinges of the cupboard with sandpaper to scratch the shiny surface and provide a key for the paint. Apply black paint to the end of a small paint roller and roll the colour on to the hinges. This will help to give a pitted texture to the paint and look more realistically like metal. When dry, apply a second coat in the same way, then follow the instructions on page 15 for the rusting metal effect.

6 Using a variety of tools, scrape, scratch and dent the cupboard surface. Stab a pointed screwdriver here and there to create small holes and use a hammer to round off all sharp edges. Apply this treatment to the unpainted top surface at the same time.

8 Rub a ball of 00-grade wire wool over the paint to remove the masking fluid and distress the surface. Pick off some of the resist with your fingers. Then rub down with medium-grade sandpaper and remove the dust with a damp sponge.

9 Rub your hands over the surface to feel for any remaining lumps of masking fluid and pick these off with your fingers. These areas will look like newly chipped paint. Repeat step 6 and finally polish the surface with 0000-grade wire wool.

11 Replace the door fittings on the cupboard, then make any final adjustments to the distressing. Using a fine brush and woodstain, darken those areas where the wood is revealed. If you have used new screws, dab a little of the black and brown colour over the heads to antique them.

12 Finally, varnish the cupboard top with two coats of matt acrylic varnish, allowing the first coat to dry before applying the second. Apply this to the rest of the cupboard too, if you require a durable finish.

EDWARDIAN KITCHEN RACK

A decorative peeling, crackling paint effect has been given to this new, but ready-painted rack. This was achieved by applying a crackle glaze medium over a base coat of bright blue paint, then painting lighter shades of blue emulsion over the dry glaze.

YOU WILL NEED

Three shades of blue emulsion paint

Crackle glaze

5cm (2in) paintbrush

Masking tape

Satin or matt acrylic varnish

Varnish brush

This hanging rack had already been given a worn paint effect, but it had been lying around a warehouse for quite a while and looked rather shabby. The blue crackle finish makes a good backdrop for all those attractive but dull-coloured kitchen utensils that need to be kept to hand. The deep blue cracks visible beneath paler shades look very effective, but to get a good result, the top colour of paint needs to be opaque enough to cover a darker shade in one coat. It is often easier to use light colours beneath dark ones.

Achieving this effect can be tricky, especially on such a large piece of furniture. It is a good idea to practise the technique first on an offcut of wood or cardboard until you feel sufficiently confident to tackle the project. Confidence to work quickly with a sufficiently loaded brush are the elements required for a good result.

Crackle glaze is a water-soluble and inherently unstable medium that causes any emulsion paint placed over it to crack. It can be found in most decorating stores but, as brands vary, you will need to follow the individual manufacturer's instructions for drying times. However, most brands will feel dry in less than an hour, and it is usually perfectly acceptable, even preferable, to leave it until the following day before applying a top coat. Emulsion paint is usually applied as a base coat, although this is not obligatory, as crackle glaze can be applied directly over bare wood. When the glaze is dry, emulsion paint with a good flowing consistency is effectively laid, rather than brushed over the surface. It may be necessary to add a little water to dilute thick paint. Care has to be taken not to overbrush an area already painted, as this can re-activate the glaze, giving the paint a lumpy appearance. Insufficient paint on the brush causes patchy paintwork with the tendency to overpaint the area again, so reactivating the glaze and making the problem worse. Any patchy areas should be left to dry, then touched up with more paint.

1 Remove the hooks from the cupboard and rub the surface with medium-grade sandpaper. Paint the rack with the darkest blue paint and leave to dry.

4 Use strips of masking tape to protect the crackled edges, then apply the lightest blue paint over the central panels. Carefully remove the tape, then allow the paint to dry.

2 Brush a fairly thin layer of crackle glaze over the painted surface of the rack and leave to dry.

3 Apply medium blue paint over the edges of the rack. Use a well-loaded brush to lay, rather than brush the paint on to the surface; work quickly, but try not to go over an area already painted. Leave the paint to dry, then fill in any gaps.

5 Seal the surface of the rack with two coats of satin or matt acrylic varnish, leaving the first coat to dry for two hours before applying the next. The decorated rack can now be hung on the wall and filled with kitchen paraphernalia.

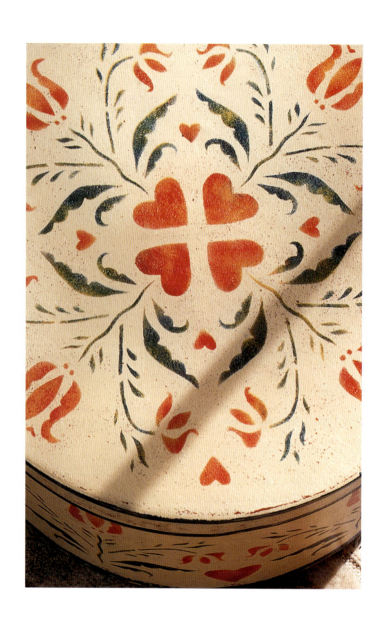

CHAPTER 2

Introducing pattern and design

Découpage, stencilling and simple freehand techniques are all used to introduce pattern to painted surfaces in this chapter. No experience is required – you are carefully taken through each process, step by step.

GEORGIAN BLANKET BOX

This plain blanket box is embellished with prints of classical dancing figures framed by gold borders to suggest panelling.
As the paint and paper backgrounds are both black, this makes it difficult to detect where one finishes and the other begins.

YOU WILL NEED

Wooden blanket box

Fine- and medium-grade sandpaper

Sanding block

Emulsion paint: vermilion and black

5cm (2in) paintbrush

0000-grade wire wool

Methylated spirit

Ruler

Water-soluble coloured pencil

Masking tape, standard and narrow widths

Narrow paintbrush

Gold acrylic paint

Scissors

Paper prints

Paper towel

Clear shellac

Wallpaper paste

Glue brush

Lino printing roller (optional)

Acrylic varnish

Varnish brush

You will need a set of prints that fit on to the front of the blanket box; if necessary, you can alter the scale of your prints to fit, by enlarging or reducing them on a colour photocopier. A vermilion paint has been used beneath the black which complements the red tones in the paper prints. The distressing has been kept very subtle and mostly to the edges of the chest, so that it is not made obvious that the background to the dancers has been painted in a different way.

Once the chest has been painted, the panels need to be marked out. The easiest way to do this is to draw a little diagram with an outline roughly the same proportions as the front of the chest.

Draw three panels on the diagram with a narrow border surrounding each one as shown below. Mark the border width as 6mm (¼ in) all round and write on the horizontal and vertical measurements of the print. Now measure the height and width of the chest and mark this down. Add the total width of all prints to the total border allowance – 36mm (1½ in). Subtract this number from the width of the chest and divide the answer by four (the number of spaces between the panels). This will give you the amount of space to be left at each side of the panels. Add 12mm (½ in) to the length of the print and subtract this from the chest height. Divide the resulting figure by two, to give you the space to be left at the top and bottom of the panels.

At this point, it is a good idea to round these figures up to the nearest 5mm (¼ in). This chest had a 2.5cm (1in) space between panels and the same space above and below them. Mark these figures on your diagram. You can then trim your print to accommodate the altered panel size. Approximately double the measurement of the width of the panel borders so that the panel size is reduced, and change this measurement on your diagram. This will allow the print to overlap the borders, thus hiding any slight inaccuracies in cutting the print or marking the panel.

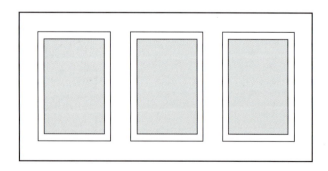

1 Prepare the chest by sanding it smooth with sandpaper wrapped around a sanding block. Brush two coats of vermilion emulsion paint over the chest, allowing the first coat to dry before applying the second.

2 Paint two coats of black emulsion paint over the vermilion layers, allowing the first coat to dry before applying the second.

3 Dip a pad of wire wool into methylated spirit and rub this gently over the areas on the chest where you want to remove the black paint and expose the red beneath, particularly along the edges. Keep the effect subtle.

4 Following the diagram shown opposite, measure the chest and mark out the panels on the side of it, using a ruler and a water-soluble coloured pencil.

6 Using a narrow paintbrush, paint the masked areas with gold acrylic paint. Leave to dry, then apply a second coat for good coverage. Leave to dry again. Remove the masking tape.

9 Brush wallpaper paste on to the back of one of the prints and stick this on to the centre of a panel. Smooth out all air bubbles from the middle of the print towards the edges of the paper. A lino printing roller helps to flatten the print. Complete the remaining panels in the same way and leave to dry for at least two hours.

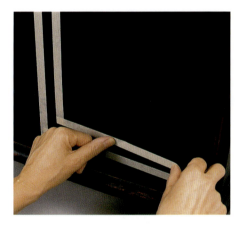

5 Apply lengths of masking tape around the outside and inside edges of each panel border in turn. These will leave a narrow central border with straight edges which can then be easily painted.

7 Using narrow masking tape, mark and mask out a border around the lid of the chest a little distance from the edge. Stick down three strips of tape next to each other, then peel off the middle length. Fill this in with gold acrylic paint as in step 6. When dry, remove the tape.

8 Cut out three paper prints to fit the panels. Dip a folded paper towel in clear shellac, and wipe this over the front of the prints to seal the surface of the paper.

10 Brush at least two coats of acrylic varnish on all visible surfaces of the chest, and at least three on the front over the paper prints. Leave two hours' drying time between each coat.

CREWEL-STYLE BEDHEAD

A crewel embroidery pattern was the inspiration for the design on this bedhead. A simple stencil forms the basis of the design and easy freehand scrolls link the leaves and flowers, making the pattern appear much more complicated than it is.

YOU WILL NEED

Bedhead

Two shades of lilac emulsion paint

5cm (2in) paintbrush

Masking tape

Fine-grade sandpaper/finishing paper

Stencil film

Permanent pen

Scalpel knife

Plate or paint tray

Foam paint roller

White paper

Scissors

Repositional spray adhesive

White chinagraph pencil

Paper towels

Fine pointed artist's brush

Satin or matt acrylic varnish (optional)

Varnish brush

The bedhead has been painted with two pretty shades of the same lilac colour. You can either buy the two colours ready mixed or simply buy the darkest shade and lighten half with some white emulsion paint. The darkest paint has been painted over the lighter shade and lightly distressed to show the base colour. The paler shade has also been used as the stencil paint. Instead of applying the paint with a stencil brush in the traditional way, a small sponge roller has been used, making the process extremely quick and easy. You need to pass the roller over a paper towel before going over the stencil, so the roller is not too wet.

There are three basic shapes on the stencil – a flower, a bud and a leaf. These are all used independently of each other, and you can cut three separate stencils if you prefer. The easiest way to work out your design is to stencil a number of motifs on to plain white paper, cut them out and then arrange them on your surface. In this way you can try out different arrangements; when you have arranged the design on one side of the bedhead panel, you can match the design on the other side. You will need lots of leaf cut-outs for the border design.

The stencilled motifs are linked with scrolling, loosely drawn lines. Use a white chinagraph pencil to draw these, so that they won't show beneath the pale lilac paint. Experiment with different shapes by wiping off the pencil marks and starting again until you are happy with the appearance. These lines are then painted freehand with a fine artist's brush and pale lilac emulsion paint, making the finished design look decoratively hand-painted rather than stencilled.

1 Paint the bedhead with two coats of the lightest shade of lilac paint, allowing the first coat to dry before applying the second. When dry, cover the recessed border with masking tape, then paint on one coat of the darker shade of lilac paint and leave to dry.

2 Lightly rub the bedhead with fine-grade sandpaper or finishing paper to distress the paintwork, revealing some of the paler lilac beneath. Work in a circular motion so as not to create scratched lines which would not look very effective.

3 Cut the stencils following the instructions on page 22, and using the templates on page 136. Put some pale lilac paint on to a plate and roll the sponge paint roller in it to coat the sponge; ensure you do not overload the roller, though, as this could cause the paint to bleed under the stencil. Then roll this colour through the stencil on to some white paper. Make several impressions in this way.

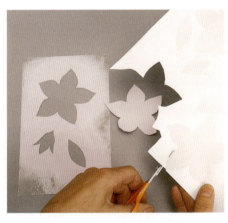

4 Cut out the stencilled leaves and flowers and arrange them over the central panel on the bedhead in a pleasing pattern. Keep trying different arrangements until you are happy with the design. Make the design on each side of the bedhead roughly symmetrical. Use repositional adhesive to hold the motifs in place.

5 Using a white chinagraph pencil, draw gently scrolling lines across the bedhead to link the leaf and flower motifs together.

6 Roll the sponge roller in some lilac paint and blot off the excess on a paper towel. Carefully position the flower part of the stencil over a paper flower on the bedhead, then remove the paper and roll the paint over the stencil. Repeat this process to stencil all the remaining flowers and leaves in the main panel of the bedhead. Work from top to bottom so as not to smudge the paint.

7 Dip a fine pointed artist's brush into the pale lilac paint and carefully paint over the chinagraph pencil lines. Complete the stencilled leaf design on the bedhead surround in the same way, following steps 4 to 7. Allow the paint to dry thoroughly.

8 Lightly rub the stencilled design with fine-grade sandpaper or finishing paper to soften the edges. Then apply two coats of acrylic varnish to seal the bedhead, if desired.

FOLK ART HAT BOX

The stencilled design on this hat box is based on a traditional 18th century Pennsylvania Dutch pattern and has been created using acrylic paints. The colours have been blended to produce a soft shaded effect.

YOU WILL NEED

Hat box

Clear shellac

5cm (2in) paintbrush

Mini paint roller and tray

Emulsion/traditional paint: red ochre, cream and blue-green

Fine-grade sandpaper/finishing paper

Masking tape

Stencil film

Permanent pen

Scalpel knife

Repositional spray adhesive

Artist's acrylic paint: yellow ochre, cadmium red and deep turquoise

Old plate

Stencil brushes

Paper towels

Satin or matt acrylic varnish

Varnish brush

The stencil was designed to fit a hat box with a lid diameter measuring 32.5cm (13in) so if your hat box is larger or smaller, adjust the size on a photocopier. By masking out the areas you don't want, you can use the design to form either a circle or a border, or you can simply use the flower motif on its own. Use repositional adhesive to hold the stencil in place. This will stop paint from bleeding under the borders.

When creating a delicately shaded stencil, the most important rule to remember is to have only the minimum amount of paint on the brush. Too much paint results in a crude lumpy appearance. Simply dab off the excess paint on to a paper towel before stencilling, so that the brush is almost dry. It is a good idea to have a different stencil brush for each colour. If this is not possible, you must wash and dry your brush thoroughly before using, or the paint will become diluted and may run.

Acrylic paint has been used for this project and this has been applied with a stencil brush, using a circular movement of the hand, rather than stippling. The paint dries very quickly, allowing almost immediate repositioning of the stencil. Yellow ochre has been applied as a base colour for all of the design; this is a very good base colour for most flower and leaf designs. The turquoise paint appears greeny-blue when combined with the yellow, and the red paint gives varying shades of orange-red.

1 Seal the entire surface of the hat box by brushing it with shellac. Allow to dry for an hour. Then, using a mini paint roller, paint the outside of the box with two coats of red ochre emulsion. Leave to dry.

2 Using the roller, apply two coats of cream paint over the red, allowing the first coat to dry before applying the second. Leave to dry.

3 Lightly rub the surface of the paint with fine-grade sandpaper or finishing paper so that the red paint colour begins to appear in patches beneath the cream.

4 Stick a stripe of masking tape around the side of the lid, leaving a narrow border at each side. Mask off a border of similar width around the bottom of the hat box. Roller blue-green paint over these borders. Remove the tape.

5 Cut a stencil (see page 22) using the template on page 137. Mask out those areas of the stencil that are not required, then secure the stencil to the side of the hat box using masking tape and repositional adhesive.

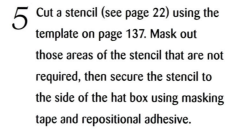

6 Dip a stencil brush into yellow ochre acrylic paint, then wipe the excess on to a paper towel. Using a circular motion of the brush, apply the colour through the stencil. Allow to dry.

7 Dip a stencil brush into a small amount of cadmium red paint and blot off the excess. Stencil the flowers and hearts, applying more paint in some areas than others. Complete the leaves with the turquoise paint in the same way.

8 Once you have completed the design, move the stencil further around the box and repeat. Continue as many times as required. Then stencil the design on the lid of the hat box.

9 When the paint is dry, seal the hat box with two coats of acrylic varnish, leaving two hours' drying time between each coat.

CHINESE CHEST

A pine bedside chest has been transformed with the addition of a simple Chinese folk design painted on each drawer front in cobalt blue. A gentle rub-down with finishing paper softens the overall effect.

YOU WILL NEED

Bedside chest of drawers

Medium-grade sandpaper

White acrylic wood primer

5cm (2in) paintbrush

Cobalt blue acrylic paint

Matt artist's acrylic medium

Old plate

Narrow paintbrush

Tracing paper

Pencil

Masking tape

Blue transfer/graphite paper

Ballpoint pen (without ink)

Fine pointed artist's brush

Fine-grade sandpaper/finishing paper

Many people feel they do not have the skill to hand-paint a design, but the technique used for painting this chest is very simple. No special brushstrokes are required and you simply fill in the design that is traced on to the drawer fronts. A ballpoint pen that had run out of ink was used instead of a pencil to trace over the design. This leaves the tracing clean, which is helpful as it has to be used several times and reversed. It is a good idea to use a transfer paper that is similar in colour to your paint, so that the marks do not show beneath the paint. Acrylic primer was used to paint the chest to provide a durable but fairly translucent finish.

1 Remove the knobs from the drawer fronts and rub the chest until smooth with medium-grade sandpaper.

2 Paint the chest evenly with one coat of acrylic wood primer and leave to dry. Paint the drawer knobs separately.

3 Mix a small quantity of cobalt blue acrylic paint with an equally small amount of acrylic medium on a plate to make a slightly transparent colour. Brush the blue paint around the rim at the top and bottom of the chest. Then paint the drawer surrounds and knobs with the same colour.

4 Trace the design on page 136. Using masking tape, secure two sides of the traced design on one side of the drawer front. Slide a piece of transfer paper beneath the tracing and secure with more tape if necessary. Transfer the design by going over the outline of the image with a ballpoint pen. Lift up the transfer paper to check that all the design has been transferred before moving the tracing.

5 Flip the traced design over and tape it to the other side of the drawer, making sure the positioning matches the first half. Transfer the design as before. Repeat the process for the other drawer fronts.

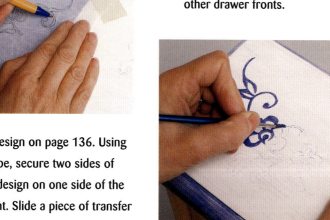

6 Mix some more cobalt blue paint with acrylic medium. Using a fine pointed artist's brush, fill in the design as neatly as you can. Work slowly so as not to smudge the paint.

7 When you have completed all the painting, allow to dry. Then, using fine-grade sandpaper, lightly sand the designs on the drawer fronts to soften and even out the paintwork. Finally, re-attach the drawer knobs.

PENWORK CANDLESTICKS

The traditional art of penwork was the inspiration for the decorative oak leaf design on these candlesticks. The technique shown here is easily approached using ready-mixed gilt varnish and a black felt-tip pen.

YOU WILL NEED

Wooden candlestick

Ebony water-based wood dye

Small paintbrush

Water-soluble pencil

Tracing paper

Pencil

Masking tape

Transfer/graphite paper

Ballpoint pen (without ink)

Gilt varnish

Fine pointed artist's brushes

Black permanent felt-tip pen

Flat artist's brush

Matt acrylic varnish

Varnish brush

Clear wax

Soft cloth

These candlesticks have been stained with a water-based wood dye to look like polished ebony; you could use black emulsion paint if you prefer. A traced design was transferred to the candlestick using the same technique as in the previous project (see page 60). However, this is repeated twice, first for the outline of the leaves and acorns, then for the interior veins and markings once the design has been painted gold. These markings should be drawn with a permanent felt-tip pen. You don't need to be too exact about the pen marks and you can even add them by eye if you are fairly confident.

Gilt varnish is used in this project, but if you prefer, you can use acrylic gold paint instead, and then omit the varnishing stage. Acrylic varnish is needed to seal the gilt varnish, which can dissolve if wax is applied over the top.

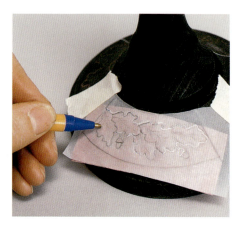

1 Stain the wooden candlestick by brushing on a coat of water-based ebony wood dye. Allow to dry, then apply a second coat if necessary.

2 Divide the base into sections and mark with a water-soluble pencil. Trace the design on page 139, then place the tracing in position on the base of the candlestick. Secure it with masking tape on either side. Slide a piece of transfer paper beneath the tracing and go over the outline of the design with a ballpoint pen to transfer the image on to the candlestick. Repeat all around the base of the candlestick.

This metal wine coaster (left) was primed and painted black, and then decorated in the same way as the candlesticks, but this time using an enlarged and straightened version of the oak leaf design.

3 Remove the traced design and the transfer paper. Carefully fill in the transferred design with gilt varnish using a fine pointed artist's brush.

4 Place the tracing accurately over a section of the gold design and secure it in position as before. Slide a piece of transfer paper beneath and this time transfer the veins on the leaves and other lines within the design

5 Remove the tracing and transfer papers and carefully draw over the marked lines with a black permanent felt-tip pen.

6 Using a fine flat brush, paint gilt varnish around the rims on the candlestick. Allow to dry.

7 Seal the candlestick with a coat of matt acrylic varnish and leave to dry for at least two hours. Finish by rubbing a coat of clear wax over the candlestick. Leave to dry for at least half an hour, then buff to a shine with a soft cloth.

GOTHIC CUPBOARD

A combination of simple techniques, including masked and freehand lining, tracing and transferring images, is used to create the stylish and unusual gothic effect on this cupboard.

YOU WILL NEED

Cupboard

Emulsion/traditional paint: dark green and crimson

5cm (2in) paintbrush

Water-soluble pencil

Fine pointed artist's brush

Masking tape, approximately 1cm (½ in) wide

Small piece of card

Pencil

Scissors

Tracing paper

Transfer/graphite paper

Very fine pointed artist's brushes

Clear wax

Soft cloth

The base of this cupboard is made from MDF, while the moulded area around the top is wooden. It is a rather unusual piece of furniture, a sort of cupboard without a door! However, its distinctive gothic elements leave no doubt about the choice of decorative style. The griffins are based on a medieval design and need to be placed accurately on either side of the drawer handle. Place the first traced design in position by eye, then use a ruler to check that the tracing on the other side is placed on an equal level and the same distance from the handle.

Red transfer paper was used for painting the outline of the griffin, as this colour is least visible under the red paint. Black paper was used for transferring the internal detail of the design over the red paint as the red paper would not show up clearly enough.

If you can find a plastic masking tape, it is possible to ease it gently around a curved surface which obviously makes painting curved lines easier. If not, draw a line around a curved arch template. This is not as difficult as it may seem as you are drawing the line only a short way in from the edge and it is quite easy to see what you are doing. Use a ruler to check that the width is roughly accurate.

1 Paint the outside of the cupboard with two coats of dark green paint and the inside with two coats of crimson paint. Allow each coat to dry before applying the next.

2 Using a water-soluble pencil, draw a line around the cut-out clover designs, about 5mm (¼ in) away from the cut edge.

3 Carefully paint the marked area freehand with crimson paint using a fine artist's brush.

4 Place a strip of masking tape down both sides of the cupboard, approximately 5mm (¼ in) from the edge. Then apply a second strip of tape parallel to the first on each side, leaving a gap of about 5mm (¼ in) between the two.

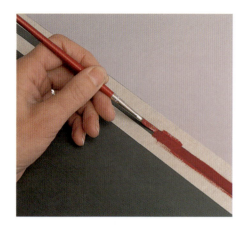

5 Using a fine artist's brush, paint the area between the two strips of masking tape with crimson paint. Allow to dry, then remove the tape.

6 Complete all the crimson borders on the cupboard, using either drawn or masked lines as appropriate. Paint the drawer handle crimson. Allow the paint to dry.

7 Cut a small gothic arch-shaped template from card, to make a border around the top of the cupboard. Hold this in place at the cupboard top and draw around it with a water-soluble pencil.

8 Trace the left-facing griffin design (see page 138), then place it on the right side of the cupboard drawer. Secure in place with masking tape. Slide a piece of transfer paper beneath and trace over the outline of the design to transfer the image. Transfer the right-facing griffin design (see page 138) on the other half of the drawer in the same way.

9 Remove the tracing and transfer paper. Carefully fill in the griffin design with crimson paint using a fine pointed artist's brush. Allow the paint to dry.

10 Replace the tracing over the painted griffin and secure with masking tape on two sides. Slide a piece of transfer paper beneath the tracing and this time trace the internal detail of the design to transfer it to the cupboard.

11 Using a very fine pointed artist's brush and dark green paint, carefully paint this detail over the griffin outline, taking care not to smudge. Leave the paint to dry.

12 Apply clear wax over the cupboard and leave for about half an hour before buffing to a shine with a soft cloth. The wax will add a soft sheen to the flat paint.

CHAPTER 3

Adding the patina of age

Coloured glazes, waxes and varnishes can be applied over decorated surfaces to add a softly aged effect. The techniques for more radically aged craquelure effects are also explained in detail.

CALLIGRAPHY CHEST OF DRAWERS

Wrapping paper with antique calligraphy and matching paint is the simple trick behind the decoration of this chest of drawers. Images of cord cut from print room sheets provide the finishing touches and the whole has been varnished for a mellow appearance.

YOU WILL NEED

Wooden or MDF chest of drawers

Woodfiller, if necessary

Fine-grade sandpaper

Calligraphy giftwrap or photocopies of calligraphy

Cream emulsion paint to match paper

5cm (2in) paintbrush

Ruler

Scissors

Wallpaper paste and brush

Household sponge

Scalpel

Print room sheets of cords and knots

Repositional spray adhesive

PVA or paste glue

Glue brush

Satin or matt acrylic varnish

Varnish brush

Raw umber and yellow ochre colourizers or acrylic paints

Although wrapping paper is used here, you could photocopy text from calligraphy books or old documents on to cream-coloured paper as an alternative. The device of matching the paint colour with the paper creates the illusion that the calligraphy has been applied directly to the chest. The chest is initially varnished with a clear acrylic varnish to seal both paint and paper and to ensure a uniform finish to the different materials. Then an ageing varnish is applied to give an antiqued appearance. The varnish used for ageing is the same clear varnish tinted with a combination of yellow ochre and raw umber acrylic colourizers. This can be used in different proportions, depending on the degree of age or dirt that is required. Build up the depth of colour, if required, by applying more coats.

1 Fill any holes and cracks in the chest with woodfiller, then, when dry, rub the surface down to smooth it with fine-grade sandpaper.

2 Paint the chest all over with two or three coats of cream emulsion paint, allowing each coat to dry before applying the next. Rub the chest down with sandpaper between the layers of paint to achieve a really smooth finish.

3 Measure the top, sides and drawer fronts of the chest of drawers. Then, making allowances for a 15mm (⅝in) gap around the drawer fronts and top of the chest, neatly cut out pieces of calligraphy paper to fit these areas.

4 Brush wallpaper paste over the back of each piece of calligraphy paper, then carefully stick them in place on the chest.

5 Using a damp sponge, flatten the paper and smooth out any air bubbles towards the edges of the paper. Leave to dry overnight.

6 Using a scalpel, trim away excess paper where it has stretched on the top and drawer fronts, and around the sides of the chest.

This writing slope (above) was decorated in the same way as the chest of drawers, using giftwrap decorated with calligraphy and flowers. The paintwork was a touch lighter to provide contrast.

7 If the paper cannot easily be removed after it has been cut, wet it a little with a damp sponge, and it should come away easily. Check that all the edges of the paper are well stuck down and re-glue any that are not.

8 Cut out and arrange print room embellishments of knots and cords on the top corners and beneath the drawers of the chest, using repositional adhesive to keep them in place. When you are happy with the arrangement, stick them down permanently with PVA glue and leave to dry thoroughly.

9 Varnish the entire chest with two coats of satin acrylic varnish, allowing the chest to dry for two hours between each coat.

10 Mix raw umber and yellow ochre colourizers with acrylic varnish to make a pale yellowish-brown mix and brush this on evenly over the clear varnish. Leave to dry and repeat this process to deepen the effect.

GLAZED DRESSING TABLE

The dressing table and mirror have been dry-brushed with several close shades of green paint and then sanded to blend the colours. A dull green translucent glaze was brushed over the paintwork to give it an antique effect.

YOU WILL NEED

Dressing table and mirror

Medium-grade sandpaper

Emulsion/traditional paint: mid-green and soft white

5cm (2in) paintbrush

Containers for mixing paint

Narrow paintbrush

Fine-grade sandpaper/finishing paper

Sanding block

Satin and matt acrylic varnish

Varnish brush

Raw umber and dark green acrylic paint

Acrylic scumble glaze

Tracing paper

Pencil

Transfer/graphite paper

Matt acrylic medium

Fine pointed artist's brush

The many layers of paint used on the dressing table and mirror, although only slightly different in colour, give a depth and quality to the paintwork, quite unlike flat paint. A dry-brushing technique is used where not all of the previous layer of paint is covered. This means there is less sanding back to see all the colours beneath. A traditional chalky paint has been used for this project; it appears much lighter when it has dried, but darkens once the varnish is applied. The colour then lightens a little when the varnish is dry. The varnish is necessary to provide a non-porous surface for the antiquing dirty green scumble glaze used for the last paint layer.

The mirror frame has been decorated in exactly the same way as the dressing table, except that it was painted with a lighter shade of the same green paint, which was made by adding white to the mid-green paint. Subsequent layers were kept lighter throughout than those on the dressing table, which makes a more interesting combination than a matching dressing table and mirror set.

The items were all made from MDF, apart from the table legs. However, they have been painted to look like wood, by brushing the paint in the direction that the grain would go. Moulded edges on MDF tend to become a little rough with painting, and will need to be sanded smooth between coats of paint.

The decorative design painted on the table drawer and mirror was adapted from a detail on the wallpaper design. The simple shapes were drawn on to a piece of tracing paper and transferred using transfer paper.

1 Sand the table smooth with medium-grade sandpaper. Paint the table with two coats of mid-green paint and leave to dry. Brush the paint across the width of the tabletop and sides and vertically down the legs. Sand the moulded edges smooth when the paint has dried.

2 Mix some white paint with the green and with very little paint on the bristles, dry-brush this over the table in the same direction as before.

3 Add some more white paint to the mix and, again, dry-brush this over the table in the same way.

4 Using a narrow brush, paint a coat of the mid-green base colour over the moulding on the tabletop and drawer edges. The finish should be slightly patchy with a hint of the base colours showing through.

5 Sand the surface of the paintwork with fine-grade sandpaper. Wrap the sandpaper around a sanding block when sanding the tabletop for a more even effect.

6 Seal the paintwork with two coats of satin acrylic varnish, leaving two hours' drying time between coats. Leave to dry.

7 Mix some raw umber acrylic paint with some of the mid-green paint to make a dirty green colour. Add some acrylic scumble to the paint mix in the proportion of 1 part paint mix to 6 parts scumble. Mix well to produce a fairly transparent glaze.

8 Brush this glaze over the varnished surface in the same direction as in step 1. Move your brush back and forth, overbrushing the glazework as you go, rather than applying it in one movement. Leave to dry overnight.

9 Trace a decorative design and transfer it on to the drawer front. Mix together some dark green and raw umber acrylic paint and a small amount of matt acrylic medium. Fill in the design on the drawer front using a fine pointed artist's brush and the dirty green acrylic paint colour.

10 When dry, seal the surface of the cupboard with two coats of matt acrylic varnish, allowing the first coat to dry before applying the second.

CRAQUELURE LAMP

This table lamp has been given a traditional craquelure treatment whereby water-soluble varnish is applied over an oil-based one, causing the surface to crack. Raw umber paint has been rubbed into the barely visible cracks to highlight them, and give an impression of age.

YOU WILL NEED

Lamp base

Off-white silk finish emulsion paint

5cm (2in) paintbrush

String

Pen

Masking tape

Water-soluble pencil

Beige emulsion paint

Fine artist's brush

Old plate

Acrylic scumble glaze

Natural sea sponge

Paper towels

Acrylic varnish

Varnish brush

Oil-based ageing varnish

Flat synthetic artist's brush

Water-soluble cracking varnish

Raw umber artist's oil paint

White spirit

Oil-based satin or matt varnish

This popular technique is, for many, one of the trickiest to master. This is because results can vary depending on the thickness of the varnish applications, the drying time left between layers, and even the weather conditions and room temperature. You may need a few trial runs before you get it right.

The technique works best on a warm summer's day, or in a centrally heated room in winter. If possible, avoid using this technique on a wet day or in a cold room, as cracking is unlikely to occur naturally in these conditions. You can use a hairdryer to heat the surface, but it is difficult to get an evenly cracked surface and often an unattractive crazing is the result. If you do use a hairdryer, make sure it is on a gentle heat setting. The size of the cracks is dependent on the thickness of the varnish applications and the length of time left between applying them. Thicker coats and a shorter time between applications produces larger cracks. Satin finish emulsion paint is used to provide a non-porous surface for the sponged glaze. The sponging gives a mottled appearance to the paintwork beneath the craquelure, and results in a very subtle appearance to the finished lamp.

1 Paint the lamp base with two coats of off-white paint, allowing the first coat to dry before applying the second. Allow to dry.

2 Measure the circumference of the top of the lower part of the lamp base, using string. Divide the length into equal sections; mark with a pen.

4 Mark a second row of dots directly underneath the first row on the bottom edge of the rim and another row of dots halfway between the two rows, with each dot placed in the spaces between the dots in the top and bottom rows. Do this by eye as accurately as you can, although slight discrepancies don't really matter.

3 Replace the string around the lower part of the lamp base, securing one end with tape. Using a water-soluble pencil, mark the lamp with dots to match the dots on the string.

5 Join up the rows of dots using a water-soluble pencil. This will create a pattern consisting of a series of triangles and diamonds.

6 Draw a triangle design around the top of the lamp, again using the string and dot technique, as before. This time mark only two rows of dots, the second row positioned on the bottom of the band, with each dot in between the dots in the top row. Join these dots up to create triangles.

7 Fill in the diamond shapes on the bottom of the lamp with beige emulsion paint using a fine artist's brush. Complete alternate diamond shapes at the top in the same way and leave to dry.

8 Put some beige paint on a plate and add scumble glaze in the proportion of 6 parts glaze to 1 part paint. Dip a damp sponge into the paint and wipe off the excess on to a paper towel. Dab the sponge over the lamp base, giving it a soft mottled appearance. Leave to dry for at least four hours.

9 Seal the surface with a coat of acrylic varnish and leave to dry for at least two hours.

10 Brush a coat of oil-based ageing varnish over the surface to cover completely. Leave to dry for between two and four hours, until the surface feels dry when you rub your fingers over it, but is still just tacky when you press your knuckle on to it.

11 Brush water-soluble cracking varnish over the surface. After half an hour, the varnish should be dry and the surface cracked. Check for any areas you may have missed and carefully touch these up with a little more cracking varnish. Leave to dry completely.

12 Dilute some raw umber artist's oil paint with a little white spirit, and rub this on to the cracked surface with a paper towel. Wipe off any excess, leaving the paint in the cracks. Leave to dry overnight.

13 Seal the lamp with two coats of satin or matt oil-based varnish. Refer to the manufacturer's instructions for the drying time.

DECOUPAGED STORAGE JARS

A giftwrap with a pretty 'salad days' design has been découpaged on these kitchen pots. One of the new two-part water-based craquelure varnishes is used to antique the design.

YOU WILL NEED

Enamel pots

Metal/tile primer

5cm (2in) paintbrush

Emulsion/traditional paint: off-white and yellow-green

Narrow paintbrush

Giftwrap or photocopied motifs

Clear shellac

Paper towels

Scalpel knife

Cutting mat or piece of card

Sharp manicure scissors

Repositional spray adhesive

PVA glue

Glue brush

Household sponge

Satin acrylic varnish

Varnish brush

Matt or satin acrylic varnish

2-part water-based craquelure kit

Flat synthetic artist's brush

Raw umber artist's oil paint

White spirit

There are several two-part water-based craquelure products on the market, and you will need to follow the individual manufacturer's advice where it differs from the general technique described here. The beauty of this water-based method of craquelure is that it is almost foolproof. However, it does not have the delicate look of the traditional technique and the cracks are generally smaller, deeper and more uniform in size. The difference between the two methods is that drying times are not critical, and room temperature is irrelevant. The pots are simply left until they are dry, usually within an hour. Raw umber oil paint is also rubbed in the cracks and left to dry overnight, but then an acrylic varnish can be used to seal the surface. Brush this varnish over quickly; don't work it in with the brush or overbrush too much or you may disturb the surface.

The paper used for the découpaged design needs to be sealed with shellac which makes it water resistant and protects the surface from damage. When arranging a design like this, it is a good idea to cut out more motifs than you think you will need, so that you can try out different arrangements. There are many beautiful giftwraps available and you are sure to find something that you like. If you are unable to find one with fruit or vegetables, try photocopying them from books of copyright-free black and white designs (see Suppliers on page 140) and colour them in.

The same primer that is used for priming the surface of tiles before painting them is also very good for priming enamel. You can then paint it with emulsion or traditional paint in the usual way.

1 Prime the enamel pots with an appropriate metal/tile primer following the manufacturer's instructions, then paint the pots with two coats of off-white paint and leave to dry.

2 Carefully brush a coat of yellow-green paint around the rim of the pot lids using a narrow paintbrush. Allow to dry.

3 Seal the giftwrap or photocopied motifs by applying a coat of clear shellac over the surface using a folded paper towel.

4 When dry, place the giftwrap on a cutting mat to protect the surface and cut out the paper motifs roughly with a scalpel. Trim them more carefully using manicure scissors.

6 Brush between three and ten coats of satin acrylic varnish over the pots, depending on the finish you require. Leave at least two hours' drying time between each coat.

8 Mix some raw umber artist's oil paint with a little white spirit and rub this on to the surface of the pots with a scrunched-up paper towel. Take a clean paper towel and wipe off the excess, leaving the paint remaining in the cracks. Leave the pots to dry overnight.

5 Arrange the motifs around the pots, using repositional adhesive to hold the design in place. Remove one or two motifs at a time from one pot, brush PVA glue in their place, then stick the prints firmly back in position over the glue. Repeat to stick down all the motifs. Carefully wipe off excess glue with a damp sponge and leave to dry for at least two hours.

7 Apply the base coat of craquelure over each pot and leave to dry. Brush on the top coat of craquelure. When this is dry the surface will be covered in cracks.

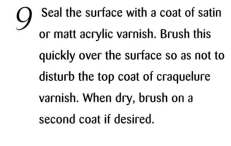

9 Seal the surface with a coat of satin or matt acrylic varnish. Brush this quickly over the surface so as not to disturb the top coat of craquelure varnish. When dry, brush on a second coat if desired.

WAXED TIMBER CUPBOARD

This cupboard has been given a patina of age using one of the easiest and quickest antiquing techniques available. A brown wax is simply applied over the paintwork and wooden top to darken both surfaces.

YOU WILL NEED

Cupboard

Woodfiller

Medium-grade sandpaper

Sanding block

Shellac sanding sealer

5cm (2in) paintbrush

Emulsion/traditional paint: mint green and pale blue

Narrow paintbrush

Fine-grade sandpaper/finishing paper

Matt acrylic varnish

Varnish brush

Dark oak coloured wax

Soft cloths

Although new, this cupboard has been made from recycled old wood. The imperfections in the old timber and its colour help make the piece of furniture look old before you start. The dark oak wax that is used over the paintwork and the wood will emphasize these imperfections, so if there are any gaps and holes you don't like the look off, you will need to fill them first. Shellac sanding sealer will help prevent stains soaking into the wood on the worksurface. It is not necessary on old wood beneath paint. However, it will make a less porous surface for the paint and make it easier to strip off the colour in the future.

Dark wax can make pale shades of paint look too brown, especially traditional chalky paint, which is very porous. Sealing the paint with matt varnish will prevent this, and make the surface more durable for kitchen use.

1 Fill any gaps and holes in the cupboard with woodfiller. Then sand the cupboard smooth with medium-grade sandpaper wrapped around a sanding block. Seal all the surfaces of the cupboard by brushing on a coat of shellac sanding sealer. Leave to dry thoroughly.

2 Paint the lower part of the cupboard with two coats of mint green paint, allowing the first coat to dry before applying the second. Leave the worktop surface unpainted.

3 Using a narrow brush, paint the moulded areas on the door, the side panels and the drawer fronts with a coat of pale blue paint.

4 Sand the paintwork on the cupboard using fine-grade sandpaper, so that some of the wood shows beneath the green paint and some of the green paint is visible under the blue. Keep the effect subtle, paying particular attention to areas of natural wear.

5 Seal the painted surface with two coats of matt acrylic varnish, allowing the first coat to dry before applying the second. Leave to dry for at least two hours.

6 Using a soft cloth, rub dark oak wax over the paintwork. Leave for half an hour then buff to a shine with a clean soft cloth. Apply a generous coat of the same wax to the worktop.

CHAPTER 4

Decorative gilding

The beauty of gilded surfaces is timeless and it can be a simple way to enliven dull pieces. You can choose between a bright shiny metal finish or a more subtle effect where the surface is distressed or toned down. The gilding process can be much easier to achieve than it appears.

REGENCY FRAME

A fine metallic gold powder has been dusted over a tacky water-based size to gild the decorative detail on this frame. This easy technique of gilding intricately carved or cast items is known as bronzing.

YOU WILL NEED

Carved frame

5cm (2in) paintbrush

Acrylic primer

Off-white emulsion paint

Small synthetic brush

Acrylic gold size

Protective face mask

Bronzing powder

Soft brushes

Soft cloth

Methylated spirit

Clear shellac

Clear liquid wax

Rottenstone

The new inexpensive frame is based on a 19th-century design and was already gilded and heavily antiqued. A lighter appearance has been given to the frame by painting it white and gilding only the relief decoration and sides of the frame.

You will need to take care that the fine bronzing powder is kept within as small an area as possible. If you are too free and easy with the application you may find a fine dust of gold powder all over your furniture.

Acrylic size is brushed thinly over the painted surface that is to be gilded. This size appears milky when first applied, but becomes transparent as it dries. This is hard to see when working over white paint, but it should be ready for gilding over after about fifteen minutes; it can be left for several hours or even overnight if you prefer, as the size stays tacky almost indefinitely. Once you have dusted over the bronzing powder, it is important that you remove as much of the loose powder as you can or it will make the paint surface glisten and spoil the finished effect.

The gilded surface is then gently rubbed with a rag soaked in methylated spirit to remove a little of the powder, thereby revealing a hint of the white colour beneath. If the white painted area is not as you wish, after you have sealed the powder with shellac you can improve the appearance by painting over with more white paint, being careful to avoid the gilded areas. Both the paint and the gilding are then softly antiqued by applying a clear wax coloured with rottenstone.

1 Paint the frame with acrylic primer. When dry, brush two coats of off-white emulsion paint over the frame, allowing the first coat to dry before applying the second. Leave to dry.

3 Wearing a protective face mask, dust a little bronzing powder at a time over the sized areas using a small soft brush.

2 Using a small synthetic brush, paint the raised relief areas of the frame with acrylic gold size and leave to dry for about fifteen minutes.

Bronze powder was dusted over a red ochre base on this candlestick (right). The finish was rubbed down and sealed with shellac.

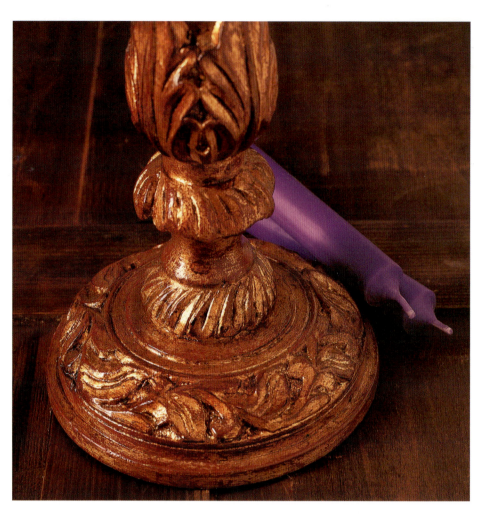

4 Dust off the excess bronzing powder with a larger soft brush, removing as much of the powder as you can. This is best done outdoors.

5 Wipe a soft cloth dipped in methylated spirit over the raised surfaces of the frame. This will remove some of the gold powder, leaving a touch of white paint showing through.

6 Seal the gilded area by brushing over a coat of clear shellac using a small synthetic brush to avoid brushmarks. Leave this to dry.

7 Mix a small amount of rottenstone with some clear liquid wax and brush this over both the gilded and the painted areas of the frame. Leave to dry for about half an hour, then polish with a soft cloth.

GILT CHAIR

A very simple gilding technique has been used to give a plush look to this elegant metal chair. The final effect is of an old chair that has been given a new lease of life. Decorated first with a rusting metal base, then with random patches of shiny gold and finally complemented by the rich colours of the cushion, the chair takes on a stylish contemporary look, ideal for the modern home.

YOU WILL NEED

Metal chair

Emulsion paint: black, dark brown, medium brown and rust

2.5cm (1in) paintbrush

Flat synthetic brush

Oil-based gold size

Imitation gold transfer metal leaf

Scissors

Stencil brush

This inexpensive chair was imported from the Far East and, as it had already been given an antique paint effect, there was no need to use a metal primer. Three shades of brown paint are stippled over black paint to give a rusting metal base to the chair. This is then covered with patchy areas of gilding using transfer metal leaf, which is crumpled to encourage the formation of gaps in the coverage for a more uneven finish. The metal leaf is applied over oil-based gold size which, once hardened, is more durable than acrylic size. Oil-based size does not remain tacky, unlike acrylic size, and therefore it does not have to be sealed. This allows the leaf to remain a brilliant gold colour, although it may tarnish with time. If you wish to seal the chair, however, you can do so with transparent shellac for maximum shine. You will find the chair easier to handle if you undertake the gilding process in two stages. This also gives you time to complete the gilding before the size becomes too dry.

1 Give the chair the ageing metal treatment as described on page 15, but omit the varnish and rottenstone step. Leave to dry.

When the size is ready to take the leaf it should feel tacky but not sticky when you press your knuckle against it and dry when you brush your fingers over the surface.

2 Brush gold size on to the top half of the chair and leave it for two or three hours under normal temperatures, then test for dryness.

The candelabra (below) was given the same rusting metal effect and gilding as used on the chair.

3 Crumple a sheet of transfer metal leaf in your hand, then unfold it carefully and cut it into three strips with a pair of scissors.

4 Press one strip at a time over the tacky size to transfer the metal, then carefully remove the backing paper. Continue in this way until you have covered all of the sized area with imitation gold leaf. Fragments of gold remaining on the backing sheet can be used to fill in small areas on the chair where necessary.

5 Using a stencil brush, gently dust off all loose fragments of leaf. Care is needed at this stage to avoid damaging the gold as the size will still be soft. Alternatively, wait overnight for the size to harden before dusting off. Repeat steps 2 to 5 to gild the lower half of the chair.

GILDED CANDLESTICKS

Transparent coloured glazes have been used to tone down the appearance of newly applied leaf on these candlesticks. Bright colours, rather than muted brown shades have been used in keeping with the contemporary designs.

YOU WILL NEED

Wooden candlesticks

Small flat synthetic paintbrush

Acrylic gold size

Copper, aluminium and imitation gold metal leaf

Scissors (optional)

Cotton wool

Blue-green and lilac acrylic paint

Matt acrylic medium

Saucer or paint palette

Soft brush

Natural sea sponge

Stencil brush

Metal leaf is available in copper and aluminium, as well as shades of gold. This project uses the leaf in loose form rather than the transfer variety with a backing sheet. The leaf is not as fragile as you might think, and can be handled with ease. To prevent the leaf sticking, dust your hands with talcum powder.

The candlesticks have been double-gilded to ensure good coverage and provide a better finish. This is not, however, strictly necessary. Loose leaf is preferable for double-gilding, as the coating on transfer leaf causes some rejection of acrylic gold size when applied over metal leaf. The acrylic gold size is applied with a soft brush so that brushmarks are kept to a minimum.

Artist's acrylic paint mixed with acrylic medium is used to tone down the bright new appearance of the metal leaf. Many colours can be used to achieve this: for example, orange-reds look good over gold, and blue-greys over silver.

1 Brush a thin coat of acrylic size over the candlesticks and leave to dry for at least fifteen minutes.

2 Tear or cut strips of copper leaf and press these one at a time over the tacky size. Tear off small pieces to patch in any missed areas.

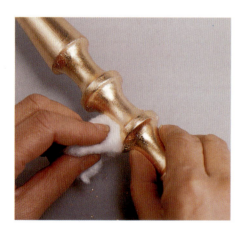

3 Using a ball of cotton wool, polish over the gilded surface and remove any loose pieces of metal. If you are going to double-gild the candlesticks, repeat steps 1 to 3.

4 Mix together some blue-green acrylic paint with a little matt acrylic medium. Use a soft brush to paint the glaze over the surface of the candlestick.

5 Break up the paint surface in a random looking way using a damp sponge. Then stipple the surface with a dry stencil brush to even out the texture of the wet glaze.

Blue and gold. This candlestick has been gilded with gold-coloured metal leaf and then a blue-green glaze was applied to tone down the colour.

Lilac and aluminium. A pretty lilac glaze has been used to tone down the brightness of the aluminium leaf used on this candlestick.

SILVERED CHANDELIER

*This chainstore
chandelier was very
prettily shaped, but had
a rather crude finish.
A more elegant
appearance has been
given by applying
aluminium leaf over a
mock Georgian, orange
gesso-type base, then
gently distressing it.*

YOU WILL NEED

Chandelier
White acrylic primer
2.5cm (1in) paintbrush
Burnt orange emulsion paint
Oil-based gold size
Soft flat synthetic paintbrush
Loose aluminium metal leaf
0000-grade wire wool
Soft cloth
White spirit
Silver-plated jewellery wire
Round-nosed pliers

Although you may pay more for a new chandelier than one from a junk shop, it does have the advantage of being electrically sound and complete, and no preparation is required before decoration. Chandeliers are typically gold in colour and the wire hooks that hold the crystal drops in place will be gold to match. These crystals need to be removed to make decoration easier; when re-attaching them to the chandelier, the wire will need to be replaced with silver jewellery wire to complement the aluminium leaf. Jewellery wire can be found in craft and bead shops or catalogues.

The chandelier was first painted with white acrylic primer, which has a dual purpose. Firstly, it primes the surface for painting with emulsion paint and, secondly, it gives the illusion of a traditional gesso surface, once thinned orange paint – representing bole, a fine coloured clay applied over gesso – is applied over the top.

The chandelier has been gilded using loose aluminium leaf applied over a slightly tacky oil-based gold size. Oil-based size is available with different drying times to reach the right tack for gilding, ranging from three hours to twenty-four hours. Japan gold size is usually dry in one to two hours. The instructions given for this project are for using a general gold size found in decorating shops, which needs two to four hours to reach the right tack. When it is ready for gilding over, the gold size should feel dry when you brush your fingers over it, but just tacky if you press your knuckle to the surface. The time this takes will vary according to humidity and temperature, but the drier the size is, the better the finish. When the size is too wet, the metal leaf will wrinkle as the size dries. If the gold size dries out completely, the leaf will not stick to it and you will need to re-apply it.

The leaf is applied to the chandelier and pressed on to the surface with fingertips. If you think the size feels almost too dry to hold the metal, you will find the heat from your hands will assist adhesion and result in a smooth and shiny surface. Once gilded, the oil-based size needs to dry at least overnight – preferably longer – to harden, before the surface is distressed. Be gentle with the leaf at this stage. Rubbing too hard with wire wool or white spirit can dull the appearance. There is no need to seal the chandelier, as aluminium leaf does not tarnish.

1 Remove the crystal drops with pliers, then paint the chandelier with a coat of white acrylic primer. It does not matter if the paintwork looks a bit patchy as this adds to the effect.

2 Brush a thin coat of burnt orange emulsion paint over the white acrylic. It should be transparent enough to see the white beneath, so dilute the paint with a little water if necessary. Allow to dry.

3 Brush a thin coat of oil-based gold size on a section of the chandelier. Leave this to dry for between two and four hours until it feels almost dry, but is still just tacky.

4 Carefully tear a sheet of loose aluminium leaf into small, similar-sized sections.

5 Place these pieces of leaf over the tacky size, one by one, pressing them down on to the surface and smoothing them out gently with your finger. This will help them to stick and smooth out any creases.

6 Repeat steps 3 to 5 on the next section of the chandelier, and continue until the leafing is complete on all sides. Leave the chandelier to dry overnight or even longer.

7 Very gently rub a piece of 0000-grade wire wool over the leafed surface, so that the orange just begins to show beneath. Do not rub too hard or the leaf will come away from the surface entirely.

8 Dip a soft cloth in a little white spirit and carefully wipe this over the aluminium leaf to remove a little more of the leaf so that the orange colour is clearly visible. Continue until all the leafed areas have been distressed in this way.

9 Re-thread the crystal droplets with silver-plated wire using round-nosed pliers to loop or hook the wire ends to secure them.

SGRAFFITO FRAME

Gold leaf and red ochre are a traditional combination that always pleases. The design on this frame is reminiscent of a gilding technique called sgrafitto, where egg tempera paint is applied over gold leaf, then a design is drawn through the paint to reveal it in gold. This design was simply drawn with a felt-tip pen.

YOU WILL NEED

Frame

Fine-grade sandpaper/finishing paper

Shellac sanding sealer

Small synthetic paintbrush

Red ochre acrylic paint for craft work

2.5cm (1in) paintbrush

Oil-based gold size

Soft flat synthetic brush

Imitation gold transfer and loose leaf

Scissors

Cotton wool

Water-soluble pencil

Ruler

Acrylic gold size felt-tip pen

Small stiff brush

Scalpel (optional)

The frame has been gilded using loose leaf over oil-based gold size to provide a smooth finish. If you are unable to obtain an acrylic gold size felt-tip pen for the decoration, use a fine pointed artist's brush and paint on acrylic gold size instead. Transfer leaf is placed over the sized design as it is simpler to apply this rather than loose leaf to a flat area. The red ochre paint is acrylic and needs to be as smooth as possible, so choose the more fluid variety that you find in a jar, rather than in a tube.

Frames are usually made to measure an exact number of centimetres/inches. When planning the design, it is easier if you make the diagonal lines every centimetre (½in) so that the design fits the frame. Although this design is simple, it is better to mark it out first to make sure it works well. This is best done with a water-soluble pencil as the marks can be removed with a damp sponge, making alterations to the design easy.

When you have completed drawing and gilding the design, you may need to make some minor adjustments to the gilding; more size than you want may flow from the felt-tip or brush, for example. Any unwanted gilding can be carefully removed with a scalpel knife.

1 Rub the frame smooth with sandpaper, then seal it by brushing on a coat of shellac sanding sealer. Leave the frame to dry.

2 Paint the frame with two or three coats of red ochre acrylic paint, allowing each coat to dry and sanding the paint smooth with fine-grade sandpaper after each application.

3 Apply gold size with a soft flat brush to the inner and outer moulded areas of the frame. Leave this for two to four hours until the size has become almost dry, but is still just tacky.

5 Carefully mark the diagonal lines of the design on the gilded frame, using a water-soluble pencil and a ruler. Ensure the lines are evenly spaced. These pencil lines will be hidden later by transfer metal.

7 Mark a simple pattern at each intersection of the diagonal lines, as shown above, still using the gold size felt-tip pen.

4 Cut the leaf into strips and press a strip over the tacky size. Tamp the leaf down and smooth it with a ball of cotton wool. Take care that the cotton wool does not get stuck to areas of tacky size. Continue applying the leaf in strips, patching in gaps as you go, until all the moulding has been gilded.

6 Carefully draw over the pencil lines with an acrylic gold size felt-tip pen, using a ruler to ensure neatness. To check that you have covered all the pencilled lines, hold the frame up to the light which will show the sized lines as being shiny. Go over any lines you have missed.

8 Cut a strip from a sheet of transfer metal, the same width as the painted area of the frame. Press this over the sized surface of one part of the frame, smoothing it out with your finger. Carefully remove the backing sheet, leaving the transfer metal in place. Continue to apply strips of transfer metal around the sides of the frame until you have covered all the sized design.

9 Remove the excess leaf by brushing it off with a small stiff brush, leaving just the gilded design.

10 If necessary, use a scalpel knife to neaten up the design by carefully scraping off the excess gilding. Take care not to remove too much, or scratch the surface. Retouch the gilding in those areas where too much leaf has been brushed off by applying more gold size, then small pieces of transfer metal, as before.

This plaque (above) was painted with two coats of yellow ochre acrylic paint, then gilded using an oil-based gold size. The background to the relief was then painted with red ochre acrylic paint over the surface of the gold leaf.

CHAPTER 5

Patinated finishes

Painting plastic to look like expensive weathered metal, plaster to look like a priceless bronze or even wallpaper to appear as embossed pewter, brings a satisfaction all its own. This is fakery at fun level, but when executed with the correct colours, it can really deceive the eye.

EMBOSSED PEWTER FRAME

A plain pine frame, a roll of embossed wallpaper and a few sheets of aluminium leaf are the simple tricks behind this old pewter effect frame. A black acrylic antiquing glaze is brushed over the metal leaf and wiped off, highlighting the raised surface and leaving a residue in the recesses.

YOU WILL NEED

Plain wooden frame

Scalpel

Embossed wallpaper

Cutting mat

Wallpaper border adhesive or PVA glue

Glue brush

Metal ruler

Acrylic gold size

Soft flat synthetic brush

Aluminium loose leaf

Cotton wool

Black acrylic paint

Acrylic scumble glaze

Saucer or palette

Small paintbrush

Soft cloth

You can order frames, made to your own dimensions, from framing shops; a plain pine one, as used for this project, should be very inexpensive. Embossed wallpaper is easy to find or you could use an embossed wallpaper border as an alternative. You need to apply the adhesive fairly generously to embossed paper, to ensure it sticks successfully to the frame. The paper will probably stretch a little when wet, slightly overlapping on mitred corners. Once the paper is dry, any overlaps can be trimmed using a scalpel knife and metal ruler, following the mitre joins on the frame.

The surface has been double-gilded with loose aluminium leaf, using acrylic gold size, to ensure good coverage and a superior surface for the acrylic glaze that is applied over it. Black artist's acrylic paint is mixed with acrylic scumble to make an antiquing glaze. This glaze is brushed over the embossed silvered surface and, after a short time, wiped off again, leaving black colour remaining in the recesses of the design. A thin layer of this glaze is also brushed on the sides of the frame; this is not wiped off.

1 Using a scalpel knife, cut strips of embossed wallpaper to the width of the frame. Protect the work surface with a cutting mat. Mitre the ends of the paper roughly to fit the angle of the frame corners. The join can be neatened after gluing.

2 Apply a generous layer of adhesive to the back of a strip of wallpaper. Stick this on to the frame, pressing it firmly into place and smoothing out air bubbles towards the edges. Continue until all four sides are complete and leave to dry. Using a ruler and scalpel knife, trim the mitred corners to neaten them.

3 Brush acrylic gold size over the embossed surface and side edges of the frame using a soft flat brush. Leave this to dry for about fifteen minutes until it becomes tacky. Cut a strip of aluminium leaf and press this over the tacky size. Smooth over with a ball of cotton wool. Cover the rest of the frame in the same way.

4 Repeat step 3 so that you have a double thickness of aluminium leaf on the frame.

5 Mix some black acrylic paint with a little acrylic scumble to make a fairly thick transparent paint. Brush this over the embossed surface and leave to dry for about ten minutes.

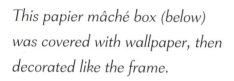

This papier mâché box (below) was covered with wallpaper, then decorated like the frame.

6 Use a soft cloth to remove the black paint glaze from the raised surface, leaving a residue in the crevices.

7 Thin the black glaze with a little more scumble, and brush a thin layer on to the inside edges and around the outside of the frame. Leave the frame to dry according to the manufacturer's instructions.

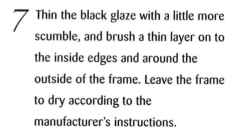

VERDIGRIS WIREWORK RAIL

A verdigris copper finish has given colour and texture to this pretty metal towel rail and shelf. The effect is achieved by building up several thin layers of blue-green colour over a metallic base, using a simple stippling technique.

YOU WILL NEED

Towel rail and shelf brackets

Metal primer

2.5cm (1in) paintbrush

Gold paint

Brown shellac

Small paintbrush

Emulsion paint: dark green, turquoise blue, mint green and white

Stencil brush

Saucer or paint palette

Paper towels

Matt acrylic varnish

Varnish brush

There are many variations of this verdigris technique which reflects the variety in naturally occurring verdigris. The towel rail has been painted with gold paint which has then been toned down considerably with dark shellac and a green wash of paint. You could replace these three colours with bronze-coloured metallic or emulsion paint, or a copper metallic paint which will give the appearance of new verdigris copper.

The paint is stippled on with a dry stencil brush. You may find it easier to use a different brush for each colour, but if not, make sure you wipe the brush dry on a paper towel when moving from one colour to another. When you are decorating more than one item, you will achieve a better match if you complete all pieces, stage by stage, at the same time.

1 Paint the rail and shelf brackets with metal primer, following the manufacturer's instructions for drying times. When these are dry, paint on two coats of gold paint and leave to dry.

2 Brush a coat of brown shellac over the gold paint and leave to dry. It does not matter if it looks uneven.

3 Make a watery green paint by diluting dark green emulsion paint with water. Brush this over the dark shellac and leave to dry.

4 Dip a stencil brush into turquoise blue paint. Wipe off excess paint on a paper towel so that the brush is almost dry, and stipple it sparingly over the rail and brackets, leaving areas of gold unpainted.

6 Stipple on diluted dark green emulsion paint to darken up some areas a little, then leave to dry.

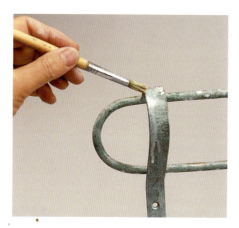

5 Make a watery green paint by diluting mint green emulsion paint with water. Brush this over the towel rail. Then, using a stockinette cloth, dab and blend the colour further.

7 Make a watery milk-like paint by diluting white emulsion paint with water. Load a small brush with the paint and let it dribble at places down the verdigris finish.

8 Allow the paint to dry, then seal it for protection by applying two coats of matt acrylic varnish over the top, allowing the first coat to dry before applying the second.

GRECIAN URN

This black plastic urn is a replica of an original Victorian cast iron one and is a perfect candidate for the verdigris bronze treatment. This technique looks particularly authentic when applied to a project that could have been cast in bronze originally.

YOU WILL NEED

Black plastic urn

Medium-grade sandpaper

Clear shellac

Small paintbrush

Large stencil brush

Emulsion paint: dark green, mint green, turquoise blue and white

Saucer or paint palette

Paper towels

Stockinette cloth

Matt acrylic varnish

Varnish brush

Black is the base colour used for this verdigris bronze effect and this makes the technique quick and easy to apply on items that are already black. Wrought iron furniture, curtain poles, candlesticks and candelabra are all good candidates for the verdigris treatment.

Smooth plastic needs its surface roughened by sanding before priming: this provides a key for the paint to adhere. If your plastic urn is not black, prime it with shellac or other suitable primer and paint over two coats of black emulsion paint. Clear shellac has been used here. Water-based melamine and tile primers work very well on plastic.

The same three paint colours illustrated on the previous project have been stippled on here with a dry stencil brush and blended with stockinette. The milky wash that is dribbled down the green paint simulates a chalky deposit and completes the weathered appearance of the urn.

This black wrought iron curtain pole (left) was transformed quickly and easily using the same technique as on the urn. For this item, however, no varnish was applied over the finish, to give a more chalky effect.

1 Rub the urn down with medium-grade sandpaper to roughen the surface, then paint the urn with clear shellac and leave to dry.

2 Dip a stencil brush into dark green emulsion paint and wipe off the excess paint on a paper towel. Stipple this paint over the urn, applying more in some areas than in others for a random effect.

3 Use a stencil brush to stipple turquoise paint over the dark green paint as before, applying the colour in a fairly random manner. Dab the surface with a stockinette cloth as you go to soften the effect and blend the paint.

4 Repeat step 3, this time using the mint green emulsion paint, and leave the urn to dry.

5 Make a watery milk-like paint by diluting white emulsion paint with water. Load a small brush with the paint and let it dribble down the urn. Apply this colour more heavily to the top rim and around the base of the urn, where a chalky deposit would naturally collect.

6 Seal the urn with two coats of matt acrylic varnish, leaving two hours between each coat.

POLISHED BRONZE BUST

This plaster cast has been gilded by dusting bronzing powder over an oil-based gold size. The gold surface is painted with gouache paint which is then polished and waxed to give it the appearance of an expensive bronze bust.

YOU WILL NEED

Plaster bust

Acrylic varnish, PVA medium or shellac primer

Small paintbrush

Oil-based gold size

Bronzing powder

Gouache paint: burnt umber and ivory black

Flat artist's paintbrush

Washing-up liquid (optional)

Soft cloth

Clear/neutral wax

When you buy new plaster castings, you will often find that they have already been sealed as it is assumed that you will not want to alter their appearance. If you are decorating raw plaster, you will need to seal the surface with acrylic varnish or PVA medium; if you do not seal it, the gold size will seep into the plaster and the bronze powder will not adhere.

Oil-based gold size has been used to give a very smooth finish to the base, which will later be polished. Bronze powder is then dusted over the size. When decorating a large object, such as this, protect your surfaces with newspaper, and wear a face mask to avoid inhaling the fine gold powder. Gently apply the gold to the surface, taking care not to overload your brush with powder. Leave the bronzed surface to dry thoroughly overnight. Failure to do this will cause the gouache painted over it to crack and peel off.

Once the gouache paint layers are in place over the gold, the paint needs to be polished so that the colours blend and the burnt umber and gold are revealed beneath the black. This is done first with a soft dry cloth, and then a damp cloth is used to highlight raised areas where the bust would naturally wear. There will inevitably be areas where you have rubbed off too much colour or scratched the surface. These areas need to be touched up with more paint and gently polished. This patching up actually enhances the finished look, making it appear more realistic.

1 Seal the bust, if necessary, with acrylic varnish, PVA medium or shellac primer and leave to dry. Brush oil-based gold size over the surface and leave to dry for between two and four hours, until it feels just tacky to the touch.

2 Dust bronzing powder over the gold size until all areas of the bust are covered, then dust off the excess. Leave to dry overnight.

3 Dilute the burnt umber gouache paint with a little water and paint this over the bust. Add a drop of washing-up liquid to the paint if cissing (the formation of globules) occurs, to help it adhere to the gilded surface. Leave to dry thoroughly.

5 Use a soft cloth to polish the surface of the paint, allowing some of the brown paint and gold colour to show through. Additional gold highlights can be encouraged by dipping the cloth into a tiny amount of water and very gently rubbing raised areas here and there.

6 Touch up areas of paintwork where necessary with more gouache colour. Gently polish and leave to dry.

4 Apply a coat of black gouache paint over the burnt umber colour, working it well into any crevices, and leave to dry.

7 Using a soft cloth, carefully apply a generous coat of clear or neutral wax over the bronzed bust and leave for at least half an hour. Buff to a shine with a soft cloth.

LEAD TROUGH

Traditional carved wood designs, cast in plastic, have been glued to a cheap plastic trough and then painted. This effective technique has given the trough a classic appearance of weathered lead that belies its humble origins.

YOU WILL NEED

Plastic trough

Plastic mouldings (see suppliers on page 140)

Pencil

PVA glue

Glue brush

Acrylic melamine primer, or other primer suitable for plastic

5cm (2in) paintbrush

Emulsion paint: charcoal grey, mid-grey and soft white

Stockinette cloth

Small paintbrush

Matt acrylic varnish

Varnish brush

Plastic mouldings are a brilliant and inexpensive way of adding classic detail to plain surfaces. You can even bend them to fit curved surfaces by soaking them in warm water or applying heat with a hairdryer to make them pliable. You will need to find a smooth-sided trough which will look more like lead, and which will allow the mouldings to be stuck in place easily. The one used here had a slightly rough texture, but if your pot is smooth, sand the surface to key it before painting.

In this technique, dilute mid-grey paint is painted over charcoal grey and dabbed with a stockinette rag to create a lead-like texture. A soft white emulsion paint is then dribbled over the surface, especially around the moulded areas, to give a weathered appearance.

If you would prefer not to buy two shades of grey, you need only buy the charcoal grey and mix this with white to make a mid-grey colour.

If you don't want to go to the trouble of sourcing a suitable plastic trough and mouldings, you can apply the faux lead technique to an inexpensive terracotta trough (below) with excellent results. Follow the same technique as shown opposite but omit steps 1 to 3.

1 Gently heat the mouldings with a hairdryer, or warm water, and curve them carefully to fit the sides of the trough. Mark the centre of the trough with a pencil.

3 Prime the trough by brushing on a coat of white acrylic primer and leave to dry thoroughly.

6 Immediately, dab a stockinette cloth over the wet paint to remove some of it and leave a textured surface. Continue around the trough until all the sides have been painted.

2 Spread a generous amount of glue on the back of the central motif and glue this over the pencilled mark on the trough, ensuring it is level. Complete the design on either side of the central motif in the same way. Stand back and check that the finished design looks balanced.

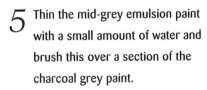

4 Paint the trough with two coats of charcoal grey emulsion paint, leaving the first coat to dry before applying the second one. Ensure that the carved mouldings are completely covered with paint.

5 Thin the mid-grey emulsion paint with a small amount of water and brush this over a section of the charcoal grey paint.

7 Make a watery milk-like paint by diluting white emulsion paint with water. Load a small brush with the paint and let it dribble down the sides of the trough. Apply more of the paint around the moulded areas where a chalky deposit would naturally collect. Allow to dry.

8 Seal the trough by brushing on two coats of matt acrylic varnish, leaving two hours' drying time between each application.

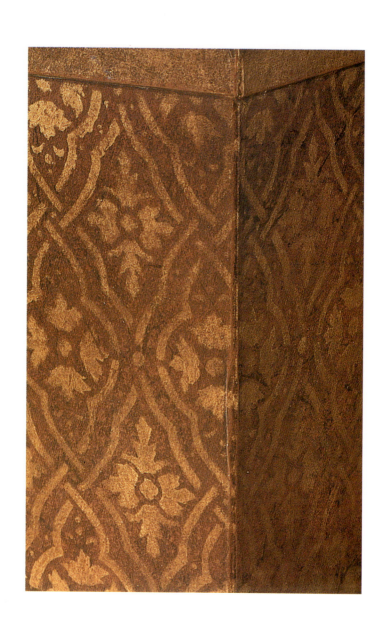

CHAPTER 6

Faux finishes

The finishes in this chapter
are classic in appearance
and are based on simplified
traditional techniques.
Surprisingly, a quick-drying
vinegar and pigment paint is
used to create elegant marquetry
and tortoiseshell effects.

STENCILLED LEATHER WASTE BIN

A 17th-century design found in a book on historic ornament provided the inspiration for this stencil design. A paint technique known as frottage was applied to the bin, using a burnt umber glaze over a tan base to create a leather-like appearance.

YOU WILL NEED

Papier mâché wastepaper bin

Clear shellac

Small synthetic brush

Emulsion paint: black and tan

5cm (2in) paintbrush

Mini paint roller and tray

Acrylic paint: burnt umber and gold

Acrylic scumble glaze

Tissue paper

Stencil film

Heat-pen and glass

Repositional spray adhesive

Stencil brush

Paper towels

Fine sandpaper/finishing paper

Masking tape

Soft cloth

Clear/neutral wax

The papier mâché bin is first sealed with shellac to prime the porous surface and help strengthen it, and then the paint is applied over the top using a mini paint roller rather than a paintbrush, giving a pitted texture to the paint. This will become more apparent when the stencilled surface is lightly distressed and help to give a leather-like appearance, which brushmarks would spoil.

The frottage technique is applied first over a tan paint and then again over the stencilled surface. The technique involves brushing colour on to a surface, placing a sheet of tissue paper over the wet paint and smoothing it over, before peeling it back and removing it. This leaves a random crinkly texture to the surface which resembles leather when leather-like colours are used. With other colours, it can also appear like worn fabric.

This is a fairly intricate stencil design, which will take a little time to cut. However, a heat-pen for cutting stencil film will make light work of it. You simply trace over the design with the hot nib, and this melts the film and cuts out the stencil. Once you have cut your design, applying it to the surface is extremely quick with only a single colour being used. You can either stipple the paint on with the stencil brush, or apply it with a circular motion of the brush. The stencilling is gently rubbed with fine sandpaper to soften the edges and give a faded effect.

1 Seal the bin by painting both the inside and outside with a coat of clear shellac, and leave to dry. Then paint the inside of the bin with two coats of black emulsion, allowing the first coat to dry before applying the second. Leave to dry.

2 Using a mini paint roller, so as not to leave brushmarks, paint the outside of the bin with two coats of tan emulsion, allowing the first coat to dry before applying the second. Leave to dry.

3 Mix some burnt umber acrylic paint with acrylic scumble to make a strongly coloured translucent glaze. Brush the glaze over one side of the wastepaper bin.

4 Frottage the glaze by pressing a piece of tissue paper over the wet glaze and then peeling it off. The wet paint will adhere to the paper, leaving behind a textured surface. Repeat this process to frottage all around the bin. Allow the glaze to dry according to the manufacturer's instructions.

5 Using the template on page 139, cut a stencil from stencil film (see page 22). Spray the back of the stencil with repositional adhesive and place it on the bin. Dip a stencil brush into gold acrylic paint, wipe off the excess on a paper towel, and apply the paint through the stencil. Continue until all sides of the bin are complete, using the outer dots of the stencil as repositional marks. Leave to dry.

6 Soften the stencilled surface by lightly rubbing it with fine-grade sandpaper or finishing paper. To prevent unsightly scratched lines appearing over the surface, rub the sandpaper in small circles.

7 Using a stencil brush, stipple gold paint around the top and bottom rims of the bin, after first protecting the stencilled surface with masking tape. Allow to dry.

8 Repeat the frottage technique over each side of the bin, following the instructions as described in steps 3 and 4. Leave the bin to dry overnight.

9 Using a soft cloth, apply a coat of clear/neutral wax over the bin, and leave to dry for at least half an hour. Buff to a shine with a soft cloth. The wax gives the appearance of polished leather.

TORTOISESHELL BOX

Rag-rolled vinegar paint is the simple technique behind this tortoiseshell effect. A lacquer red background to tortoiseshell, as used on the box, is often found on antique furniture. The frame was completed using the more traditional yellow base colour.

YOU WILL NEED

Wooden box

Lacquer red silk finish emulsion paint

2.5cm (1in) paintbrush

Fine-grade sandpaper/finishing paper

Low-tack masking tape

Vinegar

Sugar

Jam jar

Clingfilm

Small paint tray

Burnt umber and black powder pigment colours

Small synthetic brush

Chamois leather

Badger softener brush

Small flat brush

Varnish brush

Clear shellac

Satin acrylic varnish

Gilt cream

Soft cloth

You will need to use artist's quality pure pigment colour to make the vinegar paint and mix it well. Once mixed, cover the paint tray with clingfilm to prevent the vinegar evaporating and the paint drying out. Alternatively, mix the paint in a jam jar, and pour it into the paint tray as required. Both vinegar medium and unused paint will keep for a considerable time in a screw-top jar.

If the colour cisses on the surface when you brush it on, as sometimes happens, add a drop of washing-up liquid to the paint to help it adhere. Vinegar paint dries very quickly, so you will need to roll the chamois over the paint and soften out brushmarks before it becomes too dry. The marks left by the chamois vary according to how the leather was rolled and will be different each time. If the pattern is not to your liking, simply wash it off and repeat the process until it is. Paint the box one side at a time, then seal it, before moving to the next, so as not to risk damaging the water-soluble finish.

The box is finished with several coats of satin acrylic varnish to give a nice smooth tortoiseshell-like finish and gilt cream is applied to define the moulded borders.

1 Paint the box with two coats of red paint, sanding each coat smooth when dry. Protect the moulded edges on the lid and base of the box with low-tack masking tape.

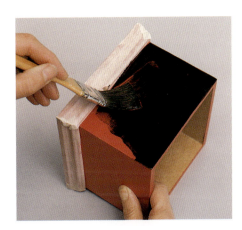

2 Mix together 155ml (5 floz) vinegar and 1 teaspoon of sugar in a jam jar. Pour some of this into the paint tray and add enough burnt umber and black pigment in equal quantities to make a thin opaque paint. Brush the paint over one side of the box.

3 Gather a length of chamois leather to make a sausage shape, then roll this over the wet paint. Start diagonally at the bottom of one corner and gradually straighten the direction up a little as you reach the top corner, so that there is some movement in the marks.

Yellow paint was used on this frame (above) in place of red. Burnt sienna vinegar paint was applied and sealed with clear shellac, followed by a second coat of burnt umber and black.

7 Using a varnish brush, seal the paint by brushing on clear shellac over the top. Leave to dry.

8 Complete the remaining sides and lid of the box in the same way as described in steps 2 to 5.

9 Apply two or three coats of satin acrylic varnish over the shellac, leaving two hours' drying time between each one.

5 Dip a small flat brush into the vinegar paint and dab it over the patterned surface to darken up some areas, providing a marked contrast in depth of colour.

6 Remove the masking tape and brush vinegar paint along the moulded edge of the box. Allow to dry.

10 Apply gilt cream over the moulded surfaces with your finger or a brush and leave to dry overnight. Buff the gilt surface with a soft cloth, then seal by brushing clear shellac over the surface.

4 Using a badger softener, soften out the rolled marks by brushing the paint in the direction of the grain, then across it, before the paint dries.

MARQUETRY TRAY

A new pine tray has been given the look of expensive hardwoods by the use of a traditional vinegar and pigment paint over which a simple design has been transferred and sealed with shellac. When the vinegar paint is removed, the design remains intact.

YOU WILL NEED

Pine tray

Fine-grade sandpaper/finishing paper

2.5cm (1in) low-tack masking tape

Ruler and pencil

Vinegar

Sugar

Jam jar and small paint tray

Burnt umber and black powder pigment colour

Small synthetic paintbrush

Badger softener brush

Clear shellac

Clingfilm

Tracing paper

Transfer/graphite paper

Ballpoint pen without ink

Fine artist's brush

Kitchen cloth or sponge

Dark brown permanent felt-tip pen

Satin acrylic varnish or matt acrylic varnish and brush

Clear wax (optional)

Artist's quality pure pigment colour is mixed with a vinegar medium to make the paint. This dries out very quickly so you need to cover the paint tray with clingfilm between applications to prevent it from drying out. Work on the tray in sections. Once you have completed and sealed the base, begin working on the sides in turn. You will find that these are much easier to complete.

When you have painted the darker border, you will need to transfer the design by tracing over transfer paper. In the photographs you may notice that graph tracing paper has been used. This is because the original design was drawn directly on to this paper to ensure it was evenly spaced and accurate. This is not necessary when tracing the design from this book, but very useful if you want to create your own design. After the design has been sealed with shellac and the surrounding paint removed, draw around it with a dark brown felt-tip pen. This not only neatens the edges, but creates the illusion of a join as there would be between inlay and surrounding wood.

This inexpensive chain-store tray was already varnished, but if yours is not, you will need to brush on two coats of acrylic varnish to seal the surface.

4 Allow the vinegar paint to dry completely. Then seal the paint surface by brushing on a coat of clear shellac. Allow to dry.

5 Apply and soften the paint around the tray sides, in the same way as the base, then seal with shellac. Remove the masking tape, then re-mask either side of the borders with more low-tack masking tape.

1 Lightly rub the tray with sandpaper to smooth the surface, then stick low-tack masking tape around the tray, where you want to position the borders. Use a ruler to check accurate positioning.

2 Mix together 155ml (5 floz) vinegar and 1 teaspoon of sugar in a jam jar. Pour some of this into the paint tray and add enough burnt umber pigment to make a thin opaque paint mixture. Brush the paint over the base of the tray.

3 While the paint is still wet, soften out the brushmarks by brushing the surface with a badger softener, first in the direction of the grain, then across it, and again with the grain, before the paint dries. This will produce a smooth surface on the paint with no brushmarks.

6 Make a darker paint by adding burnt umber and black pigment to the vinegar mix. Brush this over each border and soften as before.

9 Wash off the pigments surrounding the shellac-covered design with a damp cloth and leave to dry.

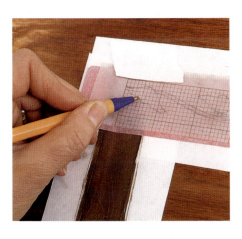

10 Draw around the edges of the design with a permanent dark brown felt-tip pen to neaten. Leave to dry for at least an hour before varnishing, or the ink may run.

11 Apply two or three coats of satin acrylic varnish, sanding between layers for a smooth finish. If you wish to wax the tray, replace the satin varnish with a matt one and finish with a clear wax.

7 Mark the centre of each side of the border with a pencil. Trace the template on page 138, then place this to one side of the centre of the border and secure with masking tape. Slide a piece of transfer paper beneath and trace over the design with a ballpoint pen to transfer it to the tray. Flip the design and repeat until you have transferred the design all around the border of the tray.

8 Remove the tracing and transfer paper. Using a fine artist's brush, carefully paint clear shellac over the transferred design. Hold the tray to the light to check for any missed areas and fill in if necessary. Leave to dry completely.

MARBLED LAMP BASE

This simple version of a grey marble is worked very quickly with a single colour mixed with acrylic medium. This technique works very well for marbling small objects and decorative accessories. Large surfaces are best left to the experienced painter as these require more expertise.

YOU WILL NEED

Lamp base

Fine-grade sandpaper/finishing paper

White silk emulsion paint

2.5cm (1in) paintbrush

Plate

Paynes grey acrylic paint

Matt acrylic medium

Natural sea sponge

Badger softener brush

Satin or matt acrylic varnish

Varnish brush

Marbling can be very complicated to execute and requires a pretty good idea of what marble actually looks like and how to handle the tools and materials used. The technique here is so simple that it should be possible for anyone to have a go. It is not meant to represent any particular marble, merely to create a marble-like effect. For this reason veins are not specifically painted on, as to do so is usually the quickest way for a beginner to ruin a piece of work.

The paint and matt medium used for the glaze tends to dry very quickly; if you find this a problem, you can add a little acrylic retarder to slow down the drying time. Work the central column and each side of the base and top separately.

1 Rub the lamp base with sandpaper to smooth the surface, then apply two or three coats of white silk emulsion. Rub each paint layer smooth with sandpaper when dry.

3 Without waiting for the paint to dry, dab a damp sponge over the wet glaze to break up the paint.

2 Mix together on a plate some paynes grey acrylic paint with acrylic medium. Using the side of the brush, paint the grey glaze diagonally over a section of the lamp base, keeping the brushmarks fairly loose and random in appearance.

4 Using a softening brush, smooth out the paint glaze, brushing first in the direction the paint was applied, and then across it. Repeat as necessary before the paint dries.

5 Repeat steps 2 to 4 on the remaining sections of the lamp. When the paint is dry, you can darken up some areas if you need to, by painting, sponging and softening as before. Leave the lamp base to dry.

6 Protect the finished paint surface by brushing two coats of matt or satin acrylic varnish over the top, allowing the first coat to dry for two hours before applying the next.

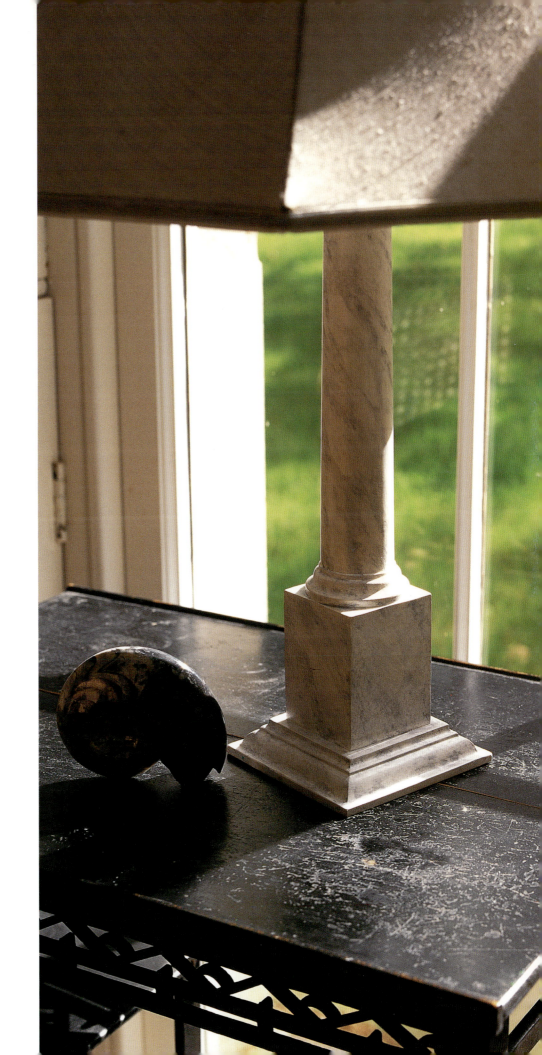

Templates

This section contains the templates for some of the projects featured earlier in this book. They are designed to save you time when undertaking any of these projects. To use a template, enlarge it to the required size on a photocopier, ensuring that you keep all the templates from one project in proportion to each other. Then trace around the template and transfer on to card, paper or whatever the project calls for.

CREWEL-STYLE BEDHEAD

(page 52)

CHINESE CHEST

(page 59)

FOLK ART HAT BOX

(page 56)

MARQUETRY
TRAY

(page 128)

GOTHIC
CUPBOARD

(page 65)

PENWORK
CANDLESTICKS

(page 62)

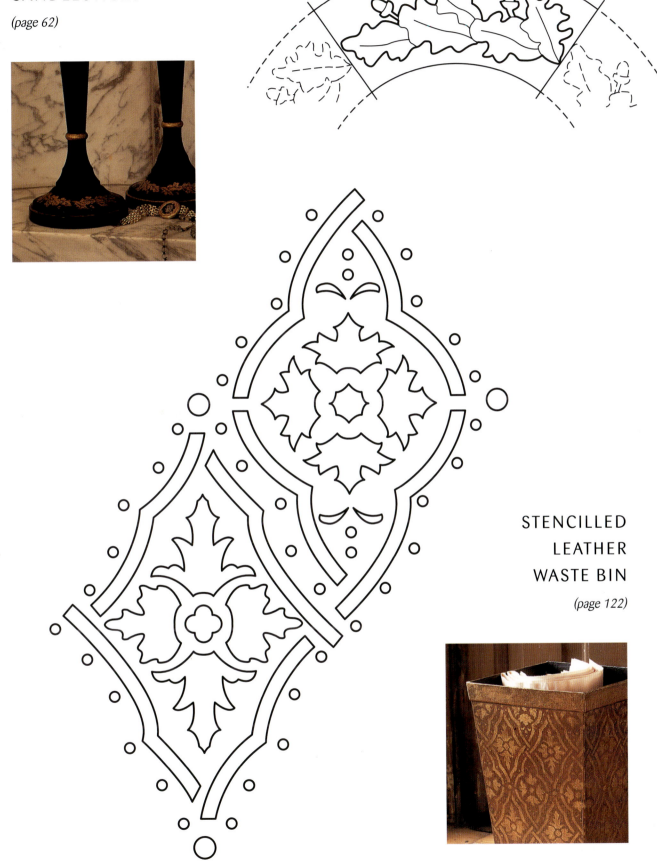

STENCILLED
LEATHER
WASTE BIN

(page 122)

Suppliers

DESIGN AND PAPER SOURCES

Caspari Ltd
9 Shire Hill
Saffron Walden
Essex CB11 3AP
Tel: 01799 513010
Fax: 01799 513101
Manufacturers of a wide range of giftwraps

The Dover Bookshop
18 Earlham Street
London WC2H 9LN
Tel: 0207 836 2111
Fax: 0207 836 1603
Copyright-free and other design books

Gallery Five Shop
8a Fouberts Place
London W1V 1HH
Tel: 0207 287 0876
Decorative wrapping paper and other products; mail order available

The National Trust (Enterprises) Ltd
PO Box 101
Melksham
Wiltshire SN12 8EA
Tel: 01225 790800
Fax: 01225 792269
Print room border sheets

Porter Design
The Old Estate Yard
Newton St Loe
Bath
Somerset BA2 9BR
Tel: 01225 874250
Fax: 01225 874251
Fine art prints

Nicola Wingate-Saul Print Rooms
Tel/ Fax: 01323 871195
Print room border sheets; mail order only

BLANKS FOR DECORATING

Amphora
155 Goldhawk Road
London W12 8EN
Tel: 0208 749 2320
Terracotta pots ready primed for painting; also finished pots; personal shoppers only – phone for opening times

Harvey Baker Design Ltd
Rodgers Industrial Estate
Yalberton Road
Paignton
Devon TQ4 7PJ
Tel/Fax: 01803 521515
Ready to paint MDF/wooden furniture and home accessories, also papier mâché items, water-based craquelure and other decorative products; mail order only

Pukka Palace Ltd
Seifton Depot
Culmington
Nr Ludlow
Shropshire SY8 2DH
Tel: 0345 666660
Wooden and wrought iron furniture and accessories made in India; personal shoppers and mail order

Scumble Goosie
Toadsmoor Road, Stroud
Gloucestershire GL5 2TB
Tel/Fax: 01453 731305
Ready to paint MDF/wooden furniture and home accessories; plaster items and a range of paints, glazes and other decorative products; mail order only

SPECIALIST DECORATING SHOPS

The following items are obtainable from the suppliers listed below except where stated: gilt creams, liquid and coloured waxes, rottenstone, raw umber pigment, crackle glaze, craquelure varnish, acrylic scumble, paint stainers, shellac, metal leaf, bronzing powder, acrylic and oil gold size, special brushes and fine wire wool. All shops supply by mail order.

L. Cornelissen & Son Ltd
105 Great Russell Street
London WC1B 3RY
Tel: 0207 636 1045
Fax: 0207 636 3655
Also a good range of art materials

Foxell and James
57 Farringdon Road
London EC1M 3JB
Tel: 0207 405 0152
Fax: 0207 405 3631

Green and Stone
259 Kings Road, Chelsea
London SW3 5EL
Tel: 0207 352 0837
Fax: 0207 351 1098
Also a good range of art materials

W Habberley Meadows Ltd
5 Saxon Way
Chelmsley Wood
Birmingham B37 5AY
Tel: 0121 770 0103
Fax: 0121 770 6512
Except coloured waxes and raw
umber pigment

Ray Munn Ltd
861-863 Fulham Road
London SW6 5HP
Tel/Fax: 0207 736 9876
Except rottenstone, raw umber
pigment and gilding material

Paint Service Co Ltd
19 Eccleston Street
London SW1W 9LX
Tel: 0207 730 6408
Fax: 0207 730 7458

Papers and Paints
4 Park Walk
London SW10 OAD
Tel: 0207 352 8626
Fax 0207 352 1017
Except gilt creams and metal leaf

E Ploton (Sundries) Ltd
273 Archway Road
London N6 5AA
Tel: 0208 348 0315
Fax: 0208 348 3414
Also a good range of art materials

Relics
35 Bridge Street
Witney
Oxfordshire OX8 6DA
Tel/Fax: 01993 704611
Also Annie Sloan traditional paint

Stuart R Stevenson
68 Clerkenwell Road
London EC1M 5QA
Tel: 0207 253 l693
Fax: 0207 490 0451
Also a good range of art materials

OTHER SUPPLIERS

Craig & Rose
172 Leith Walk
Edinburgh EH6 5EB
Tel: 0131 554 1131
Fax: 0131 553 3250
Manufacturers of paint, acrylic varnishes,
scumble glaze and crackle mediums;
phone for details of local stockist

In Arcadia
North One Garden Centre
25A Englefield Road
London N1
Tel: 0207 923 3553
Furnishings and accessories

Liberon Waxes Ltd
Mountfield Industrial Estate
Learoyd Road
New Romney
Kent TN28 8XU
Tel: 01797 367555
Fax: 01797 367575
Manufacturers of coloured waxes, shellac,
pigment, wood dyes, gilt creams and
more; phone for details of local stockist

The Looking Glass of Bath
94-96 Walcot Street
Bath BA1 5BG
Tel/Fax: 01225 461969
Antique mirror glass

Pine Brush Products
Stockingate
Coton Clanford
Stafford ST18 9PB
Tel: 01785 282799
Fax: 01785 282292
Colourman traditional paint, crackle glaze,
coloured waxes and furniture for
decorating; mail order or phone for
nearest stockist

Polyvine Ltd
Vine House
Rockhampton
Berkeley
Gloucestershire GL13 9DT
Tel: 01454 261276
Fax: 01454 261286
Manufacturers of water-borne products
including acrylic scumble varnishes,
crackle mediums and colourants; phone
for details of local stockist

Shortwood Carvings
Unit 8, Gun Wharf
Old Ford Road
London E3 5QB
Tel: 0208 981 8161
Fax: 0208 983 0629
Moulded decorations in plastic; mail order

Simply Chateau
Old Dairy Antiques
Station Road
Semley
Shaftesbury
Dorset
Tel: 01747 811699
Furnishings and accessories

The Stencil Library
Stocksfield Hall
Stocksfield
Northumberland NE43 7TN
Tel: 01661 844844
Fax: 01661 843984
Stencil supplies including brushes,
heat-pens, stencil film and large range of
pre-cut stencils; mail order

The Stencil Store
PO Box 30
Rickmansworth
Hertfordshire WD3 5LG
Tel: 01923 285577
Fax: 01923 285136
As for The Stencil Library; phone for
details of nearest store

Index

Acknowledgements

A big thank you, once again, to the team: David and Kit for lovely pics and design, Jon for his patience with the steps, Heather for being efficient and jolly, and Sheila at Aurum for her trust. Many thanks also to Elaine Green, Chris Mowe, Fiona Bennett and Judy Wetherall for providing inspiration and sharing their knowledge. Special thanks to Nick for taking over when deadlines loomed and chaos threatened.

Aurum Press would like to thank Jane and Nicholas Ostler for allowing them to shoot at Batheaston Villa, and the following companies for donating materials or lending items for photography:
Caspari for giftwrap; *Craig and Rose* for varnish and glazes; *In Arcadia* for the monogrammed French linen sheet and pillow cases (see page 52), the Ching dynasty Chinese saucer bowls (see page 83) and the pewter armorial plate (see page 105); *The Looking Glass* of Bath for the antique mirror glass (see page 75); *Shortwood Carvings* for mouldings (see page 117); and *Simply Chateau* for the French cane bench, cushions and curtains (see page 75), and the French silk tassel (see page 91). The 'Salad Days' wrapping paper used in the projects on page 81 was illustrated by Claire Winteringham, © Gallery Five 1996.